J
973.5
PRES

Presidents of a Young
Republic: A Sourcebook on
the U.S. Presidency

$14.95

DATE DUE			

PRESIDENTS OF
A YOUNG REPUBLIC

A SOURCEBOOK ON THE U.S. PRESIDENCY

PRESIDENTS OF A YOUNG REPUBLIC

A SOURCEBOOK ON THE U.S. PRESIDENCY

Edited by Carter Smith

AMERICAN ALBUMS FROM THE COLLECTIONS OF
THE LIBRARY OF CONGRESS

THE MILLBROOK PRESS, *Brookfield, Connecticut*

Cover: "Genl. Andrew Jackson: The Hero of New Orleans." Hand-colored print by Currier & Ives, nineteenth century.

Title Page: "Washington, from the President's House." Hand-colored lithograph, published by Nathaniel Currier, 1848.

Contents Page: "National Guard Half Pounds." Lithograph by Sarony & Major, 1857.

Back Cover: "Grand National Democratic Banner: Press Onward." Hand-colored lithograph by Nathaniel Currier, 1852.

Library of Congress Cataloging-in-Publication Data

Presidents of a young republic : a sourcebook on the U.S. presidency / edited by Carter Smith.
     p. cm. — (American albums from the collections of the Library of Congress)
     Includes bibliographical references and index.
     Summary: Uses a variety of contemporary materials to describe and illustrate the political and personal lives of the United States presidents from John Quincy Adams to James Buchanan
     ISBN 1-56294-359-6 (lib. bdg.)
     1. Presidents—United States—History—19th century—Juvenile literature. 2. Presidents—United States—History—19th century—Sources—Juvenile literature. 3. United States—Politics and government—1815–1861—Juvenile literature. 4. United States—Politics and government—1815–1861—Sources—Juvenile literature. [1. Presidents—Sources. 2. United States—Politics and government—1815–1861—Sources.] I. Smith, C. Carter. II. Series.
E176.1.P929 1993
973.5'092'2—dc20
[B]   93-12752
                                        CIP
                                        AC

 Created in association with Media Projects Incorporated

C. Carter Smith, *Executive Editor*
Lelia Wardwell, *Managing Editor*
Charles A. Wills, *Principal Writer*
Lydia Link, *Designer*
Athena Angelos, *Picture Researcher*
John Kern, *Researcher*

The consultation of Bernard F. Reilly, Jr., Head Curator of the Prints and Photographs Division of the Library of Congress, is gratefully acknowledged.

Contents

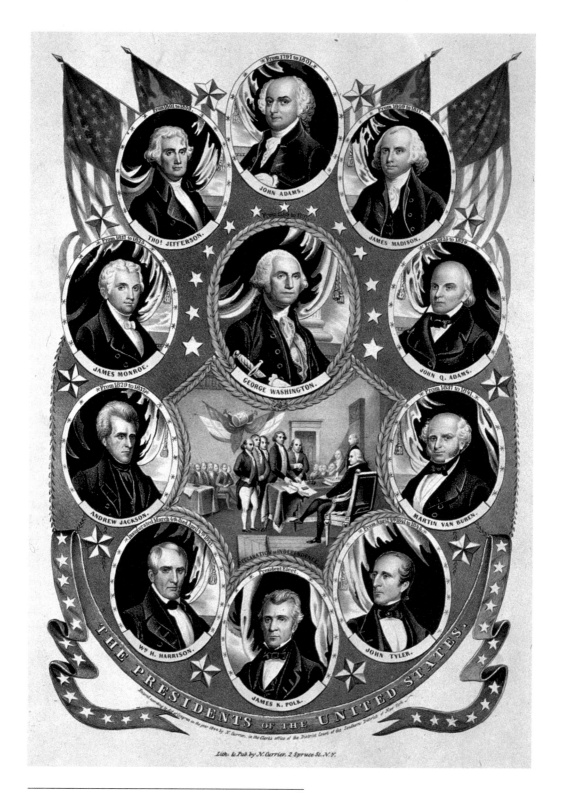

This patriotic lithograph by Currier & Ives
includes portraits of the first eleven presidents—
from George Washington to James K. Polk.

Introduction

PRESIDENTS OF A YOUNG REPUBLIC is one of the volumes in a series published by The Millbrook Press titled AMERICAN ALBUMS FROM THE COLLECTIONS OF THE LIBRARY OF CONGRESS and one of six books in the series subtitled SOURCEBOOKS ON THE U.S. PRESIDENCY. This series chronicles the American presidency from George Washington through Bill Clinton.

The popular prints, broadsides, banners, and other ephemera reproduced in this volume reveal a great deal about how Americans of the young republic perceived the presidency, the occupant of that office, and those who aspired to it. Almost from the beginning, Americans have been intensely interested in every aspect of the lives of the presidents: their birthplaces and boyhood homes, their families and careers, and even their final moments. (Thousands of copies were sold of Arthur Stansbury's portrait of John Quincy Adams on his deathbed in the Capitol).

From early on, administrations found that popular prints could be useful propaganda tools. In many cases they were designed to show how the president or his supporters *wanted* people to view the chief executive, and presented him in a favorable, if not completely accurate, light. Formal portraits of presidents often aimed to evoke the particular philosophy or character that the president brought to the office. Official portraits of Andrew Jackson and William Henry Harrison, for instance, attempt to convey a military bearing and a homespun simplicity. Martin Van Buren's sought to exude a refined statesmanlike character.

On the other hand, political cartoonists of this time subjected public figures to insults that would shock modern viewers. The Democrats, starting with Andrew Jackson and his successors, were particularly bitterly attacked in the cartoons.

The pictorial works in this volume also chronicle the process whereby American political parties battled to place their candidates in the White House. The 1856 campaign pioneered the use of the poster. Although the earliest surviving presidential campaign poster was issued for Zachary Taylor in 1848, it was in 1856 that large-scale woodcut images, hitherto associated with circus advertising, came into wide use. The Fillmore cartoon shown on page 89 is a masterly example of this genre.

More than just opportunities for the people to study the relative merits of the candidates, American presidential campaigns could and often did become grand, festive occasions themselves. The 1840 "log cabin" campaign for William Henry Harrison, a milestone in the art of electioneering in the United States, almost ignored the political issues of the time in favor of celebrating the military exploits and supposedly humble origins of the candidate.

The works reproduced here represent a small but telling portion of this rich record of the American presidency, which are preserved for us today by the Library of Congress in its role as the nation's library.

BERNARD F. REILLY, JR.

The years 1825 to 1861 were a period of growth and expansion for America. As the nation approached the middle of the nineteenth century, a new term, Manifest Destiny, came into use. It described the belief, held by many Americans, that the United States had both the right and the responsibility to expand all the way across North America to the Pacific.

In a remarkably short period of time—from 1845 to 1848, during the one-term presidency of James K. Polk—this dream came true. In 1845, the United States annexed the Republic of Texas. This action led to war with Mexico. The United States was the victor, winning California and territory that would become New Mexico, Arizona, and parts of several other states. While war with Mexico loomed, the United States and Great Britain peacefully divided the vast Oregon Country of the Pacific Northwest. In 1853, during Franklin Pierce's presidency, the U.S. bought more land from Mexico. This "Gadsden Purchase" of 30,000 square miles filled out the southwestern border of the United States as it appears today.

But expansion carried a terrible price. The question of whether these new Western territories would permit slavery had to be decided. A series of compromises ultimately satisfied neither the South nor the North. By the time President James Buchanan left office in March 1861, the United States was on the edge of civil war.

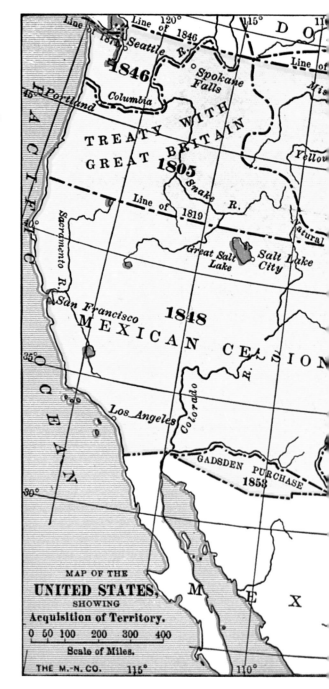

A TIMELINE OF MAJOR EVENTS
1824–1834

THE PRESIDENCY

1824 John Quincy Adams is elected president by the House of Representatives when none of the other candidates wins a majority vote in the national presidential election.

1825 Virginia senator John Randolph charges that a "corrupt bargain" led to Adams's election and Henry Clay's appointment as secretary of state. Randolph and Clay fight a duel on April 8, but neither is hurt.
• The Republican-Democratic Party splits. Andrew Jackson becomes the leader of the new Democratic party, while the Republican party is led by Henry Clay.

May 19, 1828 Adams signs a tariff bill placing high import taxes on manufactured goods from overseas to protect American industries from foreign competition.

The bill's opponents nickname it the "Tariff of Abominations."

December *The South Carolina Exposition and Protest*, secretly written by Vice President John C. Calhoun, is published. An attack on the "Tariff of Abominations," the pamphlet declares that states can nullify federal laws they believe are unconstitutional.

December 3 Democrat Andrew Jackson of Tennessee defeats John Quincy Adams in the presidential election. Jackson becomes the nation's seventh president.

May 28, 1830 President Jackson signs the Indian Removal Act into law. The bill calls for the relocation of Native Americans from the Southeastern states to a designated "Indian Territory" west of the Mississippi River, in present-day Oklahoma.

THE AMERICAN SCENE

1824 "Mountain Man" Jedediah Smith, explorer and fur trapper for the Rocky Mountain Fur Company, leads the first expedition across the continental divide and into the Southwestern part of the continent.

1825 The 365-mile-long canal Erie Canal is completed after nine years of construction; it runs from Lake Erie to the Hudson

The Grand Canyon

River at Albany, New York.

1826 John Russwurm graduates from Bowdoin College, becoming the first African American to earn a degree from an American college.

1827 On their way from Santa Fe to California, traders Sylvester Pattie and his son James Ohio Pattie sight the Grand Canyon.

1828 Noah Webster publishes the *American Diction-*

ary of the English Language.

1830 Senators Daniel Webster of Massachusetts and Robert Hayne of South Carolina conduct a ten-day landmark debate over the issue of union versus states' rights.
•The census finds that the U.S. population has grown to almost 13 million, an increase of about 25 percent from 1820. One fourth of the population is shown to be living in the

1832 Jackson easily defeats Henry Clay and William Wirt in the presidential election and begins his second term in office.

November 24 South Carolina adopts a measure which nullifies the "Tariff of Abominations." In December, Jackson issues a proclamation calling nullification "an impractical absurdity."

1833 After refusing to renew the charter of the Bank of

Cartoon of Jackson fighting with the U.S. Bank

the United States in 1832, on the grounds that the bank is a tool of the rich, Jackson removes all government funds from the bank and deposits them in state, or "pet" banks around the country.

• Jackson authorizes federal troops to enforce the "Tariff of Abominations." At the same time, Senator Henry Clay's compromise Tariff Act passes Congress. The two measures end the nullification crisis.

March Vice President John C. Calhoun resigns to become a senator for South Carolina. Secretary of State Martin Van Buren is elected vice president.

March 28, 1834 The Senate votes to reprimand Jackson for removing government funds from the Bank of the United States.

April 14 Opponents of Jackson's policies form the Whig Party.

Western states and territories.
• The nation's first regular steam railway service, with twenty-five miles of tracks, is opened to the public by the South Carolina Canal & Railroad Company.

April 6 Joseph Smith of Palmyra, New York, founds the Church of Latter-Day Saints, better known as the Mormon Church.

1831 Massachusetts abolitionist

William Lloyd Garrison begins publishing *The Liberator*, the biggest publication of the abolitionist movement.
• Cyrus McCormick, an American inventor, develops the reaper, a harvesting machine which revolutionizes farming in the United States and the world.

1832 Black Hawk's War is fought between U.S. troops and Sauk and Fox Indians over land in

Illinois. Chief Black Hawk surrenders in the Battle of Bad Axe.

1833 The American Anti-Slavery Society, the largest and most influential abolitionist group, is organized in Philadelphia with the help of such famous abolitionists as William Lloyd Garrison and Lewis Tappan.
• The *New York Sun*, the first successful daily newspaper, is founded.
• American settlers in Texas vote to

secede from Mexico. Clashes between American settlers and Mexican authorities increase.

1834 Plans for a slave uprising are uncovered in South Carolina. Thirty-four blacks are executed, including the conspiracy's leader, freed slave Denmark Vesey.
• Abraham Lincoln enters politics for the first time, joining the assembly of the Illinois legislature at the age of twenty-five.

A TIMELINE OF MAJOR EVENTS
1835–1846

THE PRESIDENCY

January 30, 1835 In the first attempted presidential assassination, Richard Lawrence tries to shoot President Jackson in the Capitol Rotunda. Both Lawrence's pistols misfire. Lawrence, who believes he is the heir to the British throne, is later committed to a mental institution.

1836 Democrat Martin Van Buren easily defeats several candidates from the Whig party to become the nation's eighth president.

1837 In one of his last acts as president, Andrew Jackson recognizes the Republic of Texas as an independent nation. The Senate, however, rejects Texas's request for annexation—incorporation as a territory—by the United States.
• The Panic of 1837, caused by over-investment in land and overbuilding of railroads and canals, begins an economic depression that is to last until 1843. Van Buren's financial policies do little to relieve the crisis, and his popularity wanes.

1840 Congress passes the Independent Treasury Act, which requires federal funds to be deposited in federal depositories rather than in state or private banks. The act, which will be

Martin Van Buren

repealed the following year, is Van Buren's major accomplishment as president.
• Whig candidate William Henry Harrison defeats Martin Van Buren in the presidential election, using the

THE AMERICAN SCENE

1835 The national debt is completely paid off as a result of revenues from increased railroad construction and skyrocketing land values.

1837 Mount Holyoke, the first permanent women's college, is founded in Massachusetts.

1838 After Representative John Quincy Adams introduces 350 petitions against slavery into the House of Representatives, the House passes a "gag rule" prohibiting congressional discussion of the issue.
• Frederick Douglass escapes from slavery in Maryland. Soon after, he becomes a powerful spokesman for the abolitionist movement in Massachusetts.
• The U.S. Army forces about 20,000 Cherokee Indians to leave their Georgia homeland and move to Indian Territory (now Oklahoma). The operation, which the Cherokees call the "Trail of Tears," is overseen by General Winfield Scott.

October Oberlin College in Ohio becomes the first American coeducational institution of higher learning.

1839 The Aroostook War, a conflict involving the boundary between Maine and New Brunswick, Canada, ends without bloodshed when American general Winfield Scott arranges a truce with New Brunswick.

1840 According to the census, the population of the United States now stands at about 17 million. The huge increase is due in part to the 500,000 immigrants who have arrived since 1830.

November, 1841 The first wagon train to

campaign slogan "Tippecanoe and Tyler, too." (Tippecanoe, Harrison's campaign nickname, came from a battle in 1811 in which the general defeated Indians in Ohio led by Tenskwatawa.) Harrison is the nation's ninth president.

1841 After one month in office, President Harrison dies from pneumonia and Vice President John Tyler succeeds him as president.

• President Tyler vetoes (refuses to approve) a Whig-sponsored bank bill, and his entire cabinet, except for Secretary of State Daniel Webster, resigns.

1842 Tyler signs the Webster-Ashburton Treaty which sets the boundary between northern Maine and Great Britain's Canada. The treaty also involves the United States in an effort to stop the slave trade coming out of Africa.

1844 Tyler approves a treaty of annexation with Texas, but antislavery senators reject it, fearing that Texas will be admitted as a slave state. The annexation issue becomes an important part of the presidential election of 1844.

1845 Democrat James K. Polk of Tennessee defeats Whig Henry Clay and Liberty Party candidate James Birney to become the nation's tenth president.

1846 American soldiers under General Zachary Taylor skirmish with Mexican troops in the disputed border area between Mexico and Texas. With President Polk's support, Congress declares war on Mexico on May 13.

June 15 President Polk signs a treaty with Great Britain settling the boundary of Oregon Country at the 49th parallel.

cross the Rocky Mountains via the Oregon Trail arrives in Sacramento, California. The seventy-person train began its journey at Sapling Grove, Kansas, the previous spring.

1842 The Second Seminole War ends after a five-year conflict. After destroying the crops of Florida's Seminole Indians, U.S. troops force them to sign a peace treaty that relocates them to Indian Territory.

Pioneers on the Oregon Trail

January 1843 Dorothea Dix publishes her *Memorial to the Legislature of Massachusetts*, urging the state to improve inhuman conditions in insane asylums and jails.

May 24, 1844 Samuel Morse sends a message from Washington, D.C., to Baltimore via the newly invented electric telegraph.

June 27 An angry mob murders

Joseph Smith, founder of the Mormon Church, in Nauvoo, Illinois. The Mormons are controversial because they advocate polygamy—the practice of one man's taking several wives.

1846 More than 100,000 people emigrate from Ireland to the United States after a disease destroys Irish potato crops. Immigration from Ireland hits a peak of 221,000 five years later.

A TIMELINE OF MAJOR EVENTS
1847–1853

THE PRESIDENCY

1847 President Polk sends diplomat Nicholas Trist to Mexico to negotiate peace terms with the Mexican government.

1848 Democrats and Whigs opposed to the spread of slavery into the Western territories found the Free Soil Party. At their first convention, they nominate Martin Van Buren for president and Charles Francis Adams (son of

Zachary Taylor

John Quincy Adams) for vice president.
• The Mexican War ends with the signing of the Treaty of Guadalupe Hidalgo. The Treaty gives a huge area of Mexico's north-ern territory to the United States. The American victory makes General Zachary Taylor a national hero.

June The Whigs nominate Taylor for president, despite his lack of political conviction or experience. Taylor defeats Democrat Lewis Cass and Free Soil Party candidate Martin Van Buren and is sworn in as the nation's eleventh president.

August 14 Polk signs a bill estab-lishing a government for Oregon Country, after much debate among congress-men about how to handle the slavery question. The final bill prohibits slav-ery in the region.

1849 The Order of the Star Spangled Banner is founded in New York. Its political wing, the American or "Know Nothing" Party, favors strict limits on immigration and opposes the Roman Catholic Church.

THE AMERICAN SCENE

July, 1847 After being driven from New York, Ohio, and Illinois, Mormons led by Brigham Young settle in Salt Lake City in present-day Utah.

March, 1848 Gold is discovered in California. In September, news of the discovery reaches the East Coast and tens of thousands of "Forty-niners" pour into the newly acquired territory.

July The first Women's Rights Convention meets at Seneca Falls, New York. The

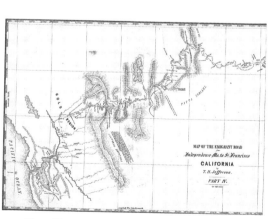
Map of the overland route to San Francisco, 1849

participants, including activist Elizabeth Cady Stanton, demand equal rights, equal education, and the right to vote.

1849 Writer and naturalist Henry David Thoreau publishes *Civil Disobedience*, an essay he wrote while in jail for refusing to pay taxes that would have supported the Mexican War effort.
• Mormon settlers organize the "State of Deseret" in what later becomes Utah.
• Elizabeth Black-well becomes the first woman to earn an M.D. when she graduates from medical school in Geneva, New York.

The Senate debating the Compromise of 1850

July 9, 1850 President Taylor dies from an infection after only a few months in office. Vice President Millard Fillmore is sworn in as president.

September Congress adopts the Compromise of 1850, which admits California as a free state and New Mexico and Utah as territories with the slavery question left undecided. It also outlaws the slave trade in Washington, D.C., and strengthens the Fugitive Slave Law. President Fillmore signs the Compromise.

1853 Fillmore authorizes a naval squadron led by Commodore Matthew Perry to sail to Japan. A treaty of friendship and commerce between Japan and the U.S. is signed the following year.

March After defeating Whig Party member Winfield Scott and Free Soil candidate John Hale in the presidential election, Democrat Franklin Pierce is sworn in as the fourteenth president. His inaugural address supports the Compromise of 1850.

December Acting for President Pierce, South Carolina businessman James Gadsden negotiates the purchase of 30,000 square miles of the Gila River Valley from Mexico. The new "Gadsden Purchase" will form the southern borders of what are now New Mexico and Arizona.

March Congress establishes the Minnesota Territory. (Its population grows rapidly, and in 1858 it becomes the thirty-second state.)

1850 The U.S. and Great Britain sign the Clayton-Bulwer Treaty, agreeing to cooperate in any attempt to build a canal through Central America at Panama to link the Caribbean Sea and Pacific Ocean.
• The census puts the population of the United States at about 23 million people.
• Mail reaches the West via an overland route for the first time. The mail is delivered from Independence, Missouri, to Salt Lake City, Utah, once a month.

1851 The *Flying Cloud*, a swift, sleek clipper ship sailing between the East Coast and California, makes a record-setting passage—eighty-nine days and twenty-one hours from New York to San Francisco.
• Novelist Herman Melville publishes *Moby Dick*, which attracts little attention from critics.

1851 The Maine legislature passes a law that prohibits the manufacture and sale of alcoholic beverages in the state.

1852 Novelist Harriet Beecher Stowe's *Uncle Tom's Cabin* is published. An attack on slavery in the form of a sentimental novel, it becomes a sensational bestseller in the North and provokes outrage in the South.
• More than 10,000 people die when an epidemic of yellow fever sweeps through New Orleans.

1853 Mathew Brady, later a major photographer of the Civil War, opens his first portrait studio in New York City.
• Surveys for the first transcontinental railroad are authorized.

A TIMELINE OF MAJOR EVENTS
1854–1861

THE PRESIDENCY

1854 When the Pierce administration is slow to heed the South's call for the annexation of Cuba, three American diplomats, including future president James Buchanan, issue the Ostend Manifesto, demanding the seizure of Cuba from the Spanish government.

May 22 Congress passes the Kansas-Nebraska Act, which organizes the Kansas and Nebraska territories and allows settlers of these territories to decide the issue of slavery—a process called "popular sovereignty." The Act is wildly unpopular in the North and leads to a widespread loss of support for Pierce and the Democratic Party.

July Antislavery politicians from various parties meet in Ripon, Wisconsin, and form the Republican Party. It later wins more than 100 seats in the House of Representatives, and control of many state governments.

1855–56 Violence grips Kansas as pro- and antislavery settlers flood the territory. Elections for a territorial legislature end in dispute, with rival governments claiming victory. Rather than trying to ensure peaceful elections, President

Violence in Kansas

THE AMERICAN SCENE

1854 Mass immigration from China begins with the arrival of 13,000 Chinese citizens. Many go west.

1855 Poet Walt Whitman publishes the first edition of *Leaves of Grass*, a dynamic, free-form volume of poetry that celebrates the American experience.

1856 The construction of a bridge from Rock Island, Illinois, to Davenport, Iowa, is completed, and railroads cross the Mississippi River for the first time. The first rail service between New York City and St. Louis begins the following year.

May 22 Representative Preston Brooks of South Carolina assaults Senator Charles Sumner of Massachusetts after the latter makes a strongly antislavery speech.

March 9, 1857 In the *Dred Scott* case, the Supreme Court rules that blacks have no legal rights and that residence in a free state or territory does not make a slave free. This ruling negates the Missouri Compromise.

October 4 "The Mormon War" begins: Mormon settlers in Utah attack a wagon train, killing 120 people, and federal troops are sent to restore order in the territory.

1858 The first transatlantic telegraph cable is completed, but the link breaks down after just two weeks of service.
• John Butterfield begins the Southern Overland Mail Company; the average journey between Tipton, Missouri, and San Francisco takes three weeks.

1859 Radical abolitionist John Brown leads a bloody but unsuccessful raid on the federal arsenal at Harpers

Pierce acts as a partisan, discrediting himself and his party.

1856 John C. Frémont, nicknamed "the Pathfinder" for his Western territory explorations, is the Republican Party's first presidential candidate. He is defeated by James Buchanan, who becomes the nation's fifteenth president.

1858 Republican Abraham Lincoln runs for the Senate

and meets Democratic senator Stephen Douglas in a series of seven debates on the slavery issue. Lincoln loses the election, but gains national attention as an antislavery spokesperson.

1860 Abraham Lincoln is elected as the nation's sixteenth president despite his lack of support in the slave states. His opponents include Democrat Stephen Douglas, John C. Breckinridge of the

breakaway Southern Democratic Party, and John Bell of the Constitutional Union Party.

December 20 South Carolina secedes from the Union. President Buchanan claims to be powerless, saying that secession is illegal, but the federal government has no legal way to prevent it.

June 1861 Ten additional Southern states—Alabama, Arkansas, Florida,

Jefferson Davis

Georgia, Louisiana, Mississippi, North Carolina, Tennessee, Texas, and Virginia—also secede to form the Confederate States of America. Jefferson Davis is elected to head the Confederacy.

Ferry, Virginia, hoping to provoke a slave uprising throughout the South. He is caught and found guilty of treason, murder, and conspiracy. Soon after, he is executed.
• Gold is discovered near Pikes Peak in Colorado, touching off a gold rush that brings 100,000 people into the territory. The Comstock Silver Lode, which is to yield $300 million in gold and silver over the next twenty years, is found in

Marines storm the Harpers Ferry Engine House, capturing John Brown

the Washoe Mountains of the Nevada Territory.

August Edwin L. Drake drills the world's first oil well near Titusville, Pennsylvania. Petroleum soon

begins to replace whale oil as fuel for the nation's lamps.

1860 The census finds the nation's population has reached 31 million, including 4 million slaves.

• Philosopher and essayist Ralph Waldo Emerson publishes *The Conduct of Life*, a series of essays on ethical ideals.

April The Pony Express begins operation. Relays of horses and riders carry mail 2,000 miles from St. Joseph, Missouri, to Sacramento, California, in under two weeks.

1861 Confederates fire on Fort Sumter, starting the Civil War.

'LOG CABIN ANECDOTES.'

HARRISON'S HUMANITY IN WAR.

THE COUNCIL OF VINCENNES,
On the memorable 12th of August, 1810,
Where Tecumseh appeared with three hundred warriors, and attempting an insurrection, was restrained by the presence of mind and courage of Harrison.

HARRISON SAVING THE LIFE OF A NEGRO.

ILLUSTRATED INCIDENTS
IN THE LIFE OF
GEN. WILLIAM HENRY HARRISON.

HARRISON'S HUMANITY IN WAR.

"Go!" exclaimed the generous Harrison, "go and take the town. But let no account of murdered innocence be opened in the records of heaven against our execrable alms. The American soldier will follow the example of his government; and the sword of the one will not be raised against the fallen and the helpless, nor the gold of the other be paid for the scalps of a massacred enemy!"

HARRISON'S ADDRESS TO BOLIVAR.

"In this enlightened age, the mere hero of the field, and the successful leader of armies, may, for the moment, attract attention, but it will be such as is bestowed upon the passing meteor, whose blaze is soon longer remembered, when it is no longer seen. To be esteemed eminently great, it is necessary to be eminently good. The qualities of the hero and the general must be devoted to the advantage of mankind, before he will be permitted to assume the title of their benefactor; and the station which he will hold in their regard and affections, will depend, not upon the number and the splendor of his victories, but upon the results and the use he may make of the influence he acquires from them."

HARRISON'S TREATMENT OF AN OLD FELLOW SOLDIER.

While General Harrison was seated with a few friends at dinner, an old soldier entered to pay his respects to his Commander-in-chief. Harrison, instantly recognizing him and shaking him cordially by the hand, turned to his guests, saying, "Gentlemen, let me introduce an old friend and companion in arms; he will take a seat at the table." The guests, one and received the soldier. He was then seated next to the General, and they all passed the evening in social conversation. When the party retired, Harrison presented the soldier with a new coat, and the veteran, overwhelmed with gratitude, bade adieu to the Log Cabin and its hospitable owner.

HARRISON PREFERRING ANOTHER MAN'S SON TO HIS OWN.

While General Harrison was Governor of Indiana, he entertained an intention of applying for a position for his son at West Point. There was only a single vacancy, and he would certainly have obtained the desired appointment. In the meanwhile, a neighboring favour applied to Harrison to exert his influence for his son, as he also desired such a place for his boy. The noble-hearted chief, ever ready to do more for others than for himself, promptly complied with the man's request, and used his influence to obtain the situation which was wanted.

HARRISON'S CARE FOR HIS SOLDIERS.

The cut represents one of the characteristic traits of Harrison, in which he is personally binding up the wounds of a soldier.

THE EAGLE OF FORT MEGS.

The General remarked that he thanked his friends of Crawford County for the present they were so obliging as to send him. Their request should be attended to; he would keep the Eagle until he could see the country restored to its liberty, either by this or any other administration; until men could go to the polls and exercise the elective franchise without fear or compulsion, by office-holders or others; until the people of this country could be free and independent, and the legislation of the country should be left to be done by the Legislature, and not the Executive. Then, and not till then, would he give the bird its freedom, that it might wing its way to its native air, and perch itself upon the tree of liberty, and be indeed the true ensign of our country's stand.

HARRISON SAVING THE LIFE OF A NEGRO.

Frequent attempts had been made to assassinate Harrison, and before the action of Tippecanoe, a negro was arrested, who was lurking near the Governor's marquee with the intention of killing him in his sleep. At the time of the action, this fellow was a prisoner in the camp. After the battle, a drum-head court martial was called to try the negro who was convicted of deserting to the enemy, under circumstances from which it was concluded that he had returned to the camp for the purpose of assassinating the Governor. He was sentenced to suffer death. The sentence was approved, and he was led out for execution, but Harrison pardoned him.

THE COUNCIL OF VINCENNES.

The cut represents General Harrison at the memorable council of Vincennes, rebuking the haughty and rebellious spirit of Tecumseh. An instance of greatness of mind which saved the people of the town from a most horrible scene of bloodshed.

HARRISON GIVING HIS HORSE TO A METHODIST MINISTER.

Many years since, while the hero of the Thames was on a hot summer evening, at the porch of his humble "Log Cabin," he was asked for shelter and a meal, by a soldier of the Methodist Episcopal persuasion. After a plain and substantial supper, they retired to rest, the good old soldier thankful to a munificent neighbour, that he was entitled to administer to the wants of a fellow creature, and the worthy minister of Christ, invoking the blessing of Heaven upon the head of his kind benefactor. Morning came, and the minister prepared to depart. He was in the act of taking leave, when he was informed that his horse had died during the night. But taking his saddle-bags on his arm, he rose to depart with thanks for the kindness of his entertainer. The old General did not attempt to prevent him. The guest reached the door, and to his astonishment, found one of the General's horses accoutred with his own saddle and bridle, in waiting for him. He returned and remonstrated, stating his inability to pay for it, and that in all probability he should never again visit that section of the country. But the General was inexorable, and reminding the astonished Divine, that "he who giveth to the poor lendeth to the Lord," sent him on his way his heart overflowing with gratitude, and his prayers directed to Heaven for blessings on the venerable Hero.

HARRISON GIVING AWAY HIS ONLY BLANKET.

During the pursuit of Proctor, all Harrison's baggage was carried in a valise, and his bed was a single blanket fastened over his saddle. This last he gave to Colonel Evans, a wounded British officer.

HARRISON'S SELF-DENIAL.

It often happened to Harrison and to his troops, while engaged in the terrible warfare which his genius so happily terminated, to suffer great privations. Frequently their provisions were so scanty that there was not enough to divide among the men. On such occasions, Harrison would not take a morsel while there was one common soldier to be provided, and the cut represents him declining the proffered food, like a generous-hearted, self-denying patriot.

HARRISON CHARGING IN BATTLE, AT THE THAMES.

One of his aids just before had entreated him not to expose his person, which was so valuable to his country, to the danger of his brave troops. Harrison could not be prevailed on to regard his own safety, but putting spurs to his horse he broke away from his friends, and was instantly, sword in hand, in the thickest of the battle.

HARRISON'S ADDRESS TO BOLIVAR.

HARRISON GIVING HIS HORSE TO A METHODIST MINISTER.

HARRISON'S TREATMENT OF AN OLD FELLOW SOLDIER.

HARRISON GIVING AWAY HIS ONLY BLANKET.

HARRISON PREFERRING ANOTHER MAN'S SON TO HIS OWN.

HARRISON'S SELF-DENIAL.

DELIVERING THE EAGLE.

HARRISON'S CARE FOR HIS SOLDIERS.

"Majestic monarch of the cloud, / Who soar'st aloft thy regal form, / To hear the tempest trumping loud / And see the lightning lances driven, / When strive the warriors of the storm, / And rolls the thunder-drum of heaven, / Child of the sun! to thee 'tis given / To guard the banner of the free."

HARRISON CHARGING IN BATTLE, AT THE THAMES.

J. F. TROW, PRINTER, 114 Nassau st.

[Entered according to Act of Congress, in the year 1840, by J. P. GIFFING, in the Clerk's office of the District Court for the Southern District of New York.]

Published by J. P. GIFFING, at the office of the Harrison Almanac, 114 Gold st., New York.

Part I

Growth and Growing Pains

The messy election of 1824 brought John Quincy Adams into the White House. Four years later, the brilliant but unpopular Adams was defeated by Andrew Jackson, the candidate of what is today the Democratic Party.

Jackson fought with everybody during his turbulent two terms—Congress, his cabinet, even his ambitious vice president, John C. Calhoun. When the Supreme Court upheld the Cherokee Indians' claim to their Georgia homeland, Jackson defied the court and ordered them removed. When the Bank of the United States angered Jackson, he brought about its downfall. And when South Carolina defied federal authority during the Nullification Crisis of 1832–33, Jackson threatened to use force to end the dispute. Despite these conflicts, "Old Hickory" remained a popular president. By the time he turned over the White House to Martin Van Buren in 1837, Jackson had raised the presidency to a new level of importance in American life.

The Whig Party, formed in 1834 to oppose Jackson, managed to get William Henry Harrison elected in 1840. But Harrison died soon after taking office. His successor, Vice President John Tyler, lacked the support of either party.

Democrat James K. Polk was the victor in 1844. Polk added almost 500,000 square miles of territory to the United States in his one term—but at the price of war with Mexico and growing tension between the Northern and Southern states.

Today, many Americans believe that presidential elections focus too much on the candidates' personalities and not enough on the issues. Some voters felt this way in the nineteenth century as well. During the election of 1840—when this poster celebrating William Henry Harrison's exploits on the frontier was published—an observer wrote that "the immense multitudes [Harrison's supporters] . . . came to be amused, not instructed. They met, not to think and deliberate, but to laugh and shout and sing."

JOHN QUINCY ADAMS

John Quincy Adams was the only son of a president to become a president himself. Born in Braintree, Massachusetts, on July 11, 1767, John Quincy was seven years old when his father, John, left home to serve in the Continental Congress, the first meeting of delegates from the colonies. In June of 1775, young John Quincy and his mother, Abigail, watched as British soldiers and American patriots fought the bloody Battle of Bunker Hill.

In 1778, eleven-year-old John Quincy sailed for France with his father, who was now the new American government's chief diplomat. He returned to America the following year, but was back in Europe in 1780 to serve as his father's secretary. He also traveled to St. Petersburg as secretary to Francis Dana, the first American diplomat in Russia. From 1783 to 1785, John Quincy accompanied his father on diplomatic missions to London, Paris, and the Netherlands.

Both John and Abigail Adams were brilliant thinkers and writers, and John Quincy inherited their talents. By the time he entered Harvard College in 1785, he spoke seven languages and had a keen grasp of diplomacy and politics. After graduating in 1788, Adams practiced law in Boston. In 1794, President Washington appointed him U.S. minister to the Netherlands. Back in Europe, he also served in diplomatic posts in Portugal, Prussia, and Sweden.

Both John Adams (1735–1826; right) and Abigail Smith Adams (1744–1818; far right) played important roles in the founding of the United States, and they passed their devotion to public service on to John Quincy. The younger Adams, however, sometimes felt uncomfortable as the son of a president. When John Adams appointed him U.S. minister to Prussia in 1797, John Quincy refused at first, fearing charges of favoritism. The president replied that "the sons of Presidents have the same claim to liberty, equality, and the benefit of the laws with all other citizens."

This engraving (below) shows how John Quincy Adams's birthplace in Braintree (now Quincy), Massachusetts, looked in the nineteenth century. Both John Adams and John Quincy Adams were born on this property.

JOHN QUINCY ADAMS: DIPLOMAT

While he was in Europe, John Quincy married Louisa Catherine Johnson (1775–1852), the daughter of an American merchant in London. When his father left office in 1801, Adams returned to his law practice in Massachusetts.

Adams served in both the Massachusetts state senate and the U.S. Senate. Although Adams belonged to the Federalist Party, he disagreed with many of the party's policies. For example, he supported the Louisiana Purchase and the Embargo Act of 1807, two policies that the Federalists strongly opposed. As a result, he lost his Senate seat in 1808. In 1809, President Jefferson sent him abroad again as U.S. minister to Russia. Adams was a skilled negotiator with foreign diplomats. He helped draft the Treaty of Ghent, which ended the War of 1812. A few years later, Adams served as U.S. minister to Great Britain from 1815 to 1817.

In 1817, President Monroe named Adams secretary of state. He served in the post throughout Monroe's two terms and scored several brilliant diplomatic victories, including the Adams-Onis Treaty (1819), which purchased Florida from Spain. His greatest foreign-policy achievement was the drafting of the Monroe Doctrine (1823). That document declared North and South America off-limits to European colonization.

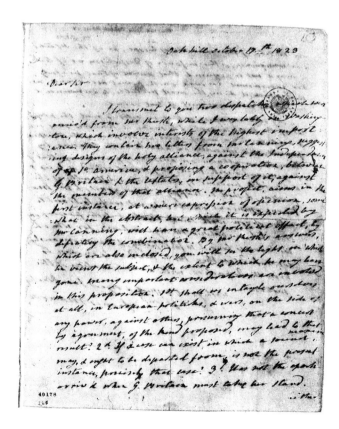

Louisa Catherine Adams (1775–1852; left) spent her early life in England and France before marrying John Quincy Adams in 1797. The couple had three children, but only one—Charles Francis Adams, who served as U.S. minister to Great Britain during the Civil War—outlived his parents. Strong-willed and independent, Louisa didn't always enjoy her life as First Lady. "There is something in the great unsocial house," she wrote of the White House, "which depresses my spirit beyond expression and makes it impossible for me to feel at home."

In January 1824, Secretary of State Adams gave a party to mark the ninth anniversary of the Battle of New Orleans. This engraving (right) shows some of the guests; from left to right, they include Secretary of War John C. Calhoun, Representative Daniel Webster of Massachusetts, Andrew Jackson (the American commander in the battle), Speaker of the House Henry Clay of Kentucky, and Adams. By the end of the year, Adams, Clay, and Jackson were caught up in a stormy election for the presidency.

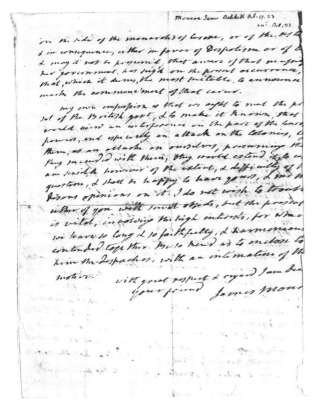

The Monroe Doctrine was largely the work of John Quincy Adams. First proclaimed in President James Monroe's December 1823 message to Congress, it stated that "the American continents . . . are henceforth not to be considered as subjects for future colonization by any European powers." Shown here is an October 1823 letter from Monroe to former president Thomas Jefferson, commenting on the proposed doctrine.

A FRUSTRATED PRESIDENT

Convinced he had the experience to lead the nation, John Quincy Adams decided to run for president in 1824. The election was a four-way contest between Adams, William Crawford of Georgia, Henry Clay of Kentucky, and Andrew Jackson, hero of the War of 1812 and now a senator from the state of Tennessee.

When the votes were counted, no candidate had a majority. According to the Constitution, the choice was now up to the House of Representatives. Many expected Clay, Speaker of the House, to emerge as the winner. But Clay gave his support to Adams, winning him the presidency. Adams then appointed Clay secretary of state, leading some angered politicians to accuse the two men of striking a "corrupt bargain." Adams was thus elected as a minority president. He acknowledged this fact in his inaugural address, telling the crowd that he was "less possessed of your confidence . . . than any of your predecessors."

But Adams didn't plan on letting this lack of support spoil his ambitious plans. In his first message to Congress, he outlined a bold program for the federal government. It should, said Adams, take an active role in building roads and canals to knit the country together, establish a national university, and promote science and learning. Adams also urged a national banking system and a tariff (tax on import goods) to help the nation's growing industries.

The lithograph shown here (above) depicts John Quincy Adams about the time of his election. In warm weather, the early-rising president liked to keep fit by walking to the Potomac River and taking a swim. One morning, reporter Anne Royall, who had been trying for months to interview Adams, appeared on the riverbank. She sat on the president's clothes (Adams usually swam in the nude) until he agreed to talk with her.

This cartoon (right) by David Claypoole Johnson portrays the three candidates in the election of 1824—Adams, Jackson, and Treasury Secretary William Crawford—in a foot race toward the White House.

Accusations of a corrupt bargain between Speaker of the House Henry Clay (1777–1852; right) and Adams angered the new president—especially because the prim, proper Adams disapproved of Clay's fondness for drinking and card playing. Clay, too, was stung by the rumors that he had made a deal with Adams. When Virginia congressman John Randolph made the charge, Clay challenged him to a duel. Fortunately, neither politician was hurt.

"OLD MAN ELOQUENT"

The new president's proposals fell on deaf ears. Most Americans, congressmen and regular citizens alike, still favored a limited role for the national government. It was a frustrating start to Adams's only term in the White House.

As president, Adams was intelligent, capable, and hardworking. But he was unpopular, and he knew it. "I am a man of reserved, cold, austere, and forbidding manners" was how he described himself. When Adams ran for reelection in 1828, supporters of his opponent, Andrew Jackson, charged that Adams wanted to make the country a monarchy and accused him of having aristocratic tastes. (When Adams bought a pool table for the White House, Democrats said he was using public money for "gambling equipment.") Jackson easily won the election.

Adams retired to Massachusetts and devoted his time to writing. In 1830, however, he was elected to the House of Representatives. He returned to Washington in 1831 and served in the House for seventeen years. Nicknamed "Old Man Eloquent" for his speeches, he waged a long battle to overturn the "gag rules"—House rules passed by Southern politicians to silence debate over slavery. On February 21, 1848, John Quincy Adams suffered a stroke at his seat in the House. On February 23, he died. "Where could death have found him," said a fellow congressman, "but at the post of duty?"

During Adams's fight to repeal the "gag rule," his supporters sent him a silver-tipped cane as a memento. Adams believed that politicians shouldn't accept presents, so he turned it over to the Patent Office for safekeeping, with instructions that it should become the property of "the people of the United States" after his death. This engraving (opposite, top) portrays House members fighting over the "gag rule." The artist, Englishman Robert Cruikshank, shows his distaste for the American democratic system in his negative portrayal of the scene.

Adams suffered a slight stroke in 1846, but he recovered and was back in the House in February 1847. But just over a year later, Adams suffered a massive stroke at his seat. Too ill to be moved from the Capitol, he was carried to a sofa in the House Speaker's office, where he died two days later. His last words were "This is the end of earth. I am content." Arthur Stansbury drew this eyewitness sketch (right) of the dying ex-president.

ANDREW JACKSON: A MAN FROM THE WEST

The man who succeeded John Quincy Adams in 1828, Andrew Jackson, was a new kind of president: a man of the people and a man from the West. Before Jackson, all the presidents, except for the two Adamses, had been aristocratic Virginians.

Jackson began his career in Tennessee, then a frontier state. His political rise reflected the growing importance of the West. The descendant of Scotch-Irish settlers, Jackson was on the outside of Washington intellectual circles, but he had wide appeal as a rough-hewn war hero.

Jackson was born on March 15, 1767, in a log cabin in Waxhaw County on the western edge of the North Carolina-South Carolina border. After serving as a boy soldier in the Revolutionary War, Jackson spent several years traveling along the frontier, working at odd jobs. In 1788, he decided to settle down in Nashville, Tennessee. Hot-tempered and fond of brawling and gambling, Jackson nevertheless became a successful attorney. In 1791, he married Rachel Robards. Four years later he bought land outside Nashville and built a plantation he named the Hermitage.

When Tennessee became a state in 1796, Jackson served as its first representative and, briefly, in the Senate. But it was in war, not politics, that Jackson won early fame.

Andrew Jackson was deeply devoted to his wife, Rachel Robards Jackson (1767–1828; above). He carried this miniature portrait of her wherever he went. Jackson's military and political duties often kept the couple apart for long periods, something that Rachel bemoaned in an 1814 letter to her husband: "You have been gon six months . . . Oh Lord of Heaven how can I beare it."

In 1804, Jackson made the Hermitage—a large plantation about twenty miles outside of Nashville—his permanent home. At first, the Jacksons lived in the log cabins shown here (opposite, top), which still stand today.

At the age of thirteen, Jackson was captured by the British during the Revolutionary War. When Jackson refused to polish a British officer's boots, the officer struck him across the hand and face with a sword, as shown in this print by Currier & Ives (right). The encounter left Jackson with scars—and a lifelong hatred of Great Britain.

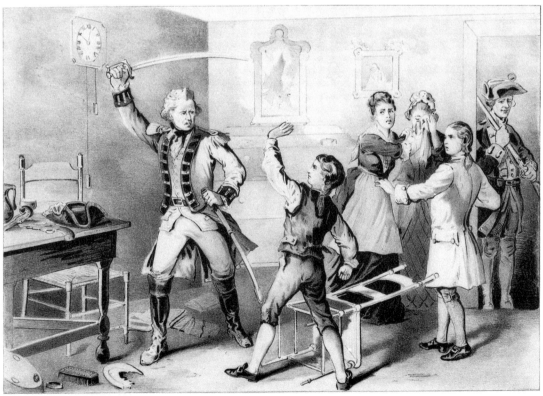

THE HERO OF NEW ORLEANS

In 1812 war broke out between the United States and Great Britain. Although he had no formal military training, Andrew Jackson was a major general in the Tennessee militia (state troops). When pro-British Creek Indians attacked American forts in the Mississippi Territory, Jackson was ordered to end their resistance. With the help of pro-American Creeks, Jackson and his 2,500 troops defeated the pro-British Creeks at the Battle of Horseshoe Bend in March 1814. Jackson followed up the victory by driving all the Creeks, whether friendly to the Americans or not, from the region. During the campaign, Jackson won the nickname "Old Hickory," his toughness reminding many of a hickory tree's hard wood.

Next, Jackson, now a major general in the U.S. Army, assembled a force to defend New Orleans from the British. On January 8, 1815, 7,500 veteran British troops marched to face Jackson's 4,500 Americans outside New Orleans. Firing from behind cotton bales, Jackson's frontiersmen shot the neat Redcoat lines to pieces. The British lost 2,000 men, including their commander, before retreating. Only thirteen Americans were killed.

It was a brilliant but unnecessary victory—a peace treaty had been signed the month before, but the news didn't reach either side until after the battle. Nevertheless, the Battle of New Orleans made Andrew Jackson a national hero.

Shown here (above) is the sheet-music cover from a song celebrating Jackson's spectacular victory over the British at New Orleans. Although outnumbered two to one, Jackson never doubted his frontier volunteers would defeat the enemy. Told that Admiral Cochrane, the British naval commander, had boasted that he would eat Christmas dinner in New Orleans, Jackson said, "Perhaps so; but I shall have the honor of presiding at that dinner."

In March 1814, Jackson defeated a force of pro-British Creek Indians in Alabama. President Madison rewarded him with a commission as major general in the regular army. Jackson also received command of U.S. forces in the Mississippi Valley and along the Gulf of Mexico. In this engraving (right), Jackson receives the surrender of Creek chief Red Eagle.

An acquaintance of Jackson's described his appearance: "In person he was tall, slim, and straight. His head was long, but narrow, and covered with thick gray hair . . . His mouth displayed firmness. The whole conveyed an impression of energy and daring." This print by Currier & Ives shows General Jackson on horseback.

THE PEOPLE'S PRESIDENT

After the war, Jackson stayed in the army. He stirred up controversy by attacking Seminole Indians in Spanish-controlled east Florida, and served as the territory's governor when it was purchased from Spain in 1821. He was reelected to the Senate from Tennessee in 1822. Two years later, Jackson ran for president but lost to John Quincy Adams. From 1825 on, Jackson got ready for the election of 1828, supported by the powerful, well-organized Democratic-Republican Party. (The Democratic-Republicans soon became known as Democrats, or simply "the Democracy.")

The election was a bitter fight, with each side making personal attacks on the opposing candidate. Jackson won, but at a costly personal price. During the campaign, Adams's backers repeated an old charge that Jackson had married his wife before her divorce from another man was final. The case was simply a legal misunderstanding, but Jackson was accused of "bigamy." The charge upset Rachel Robards Jackson so much that her health failed, and she died.

Jackson's inauguration was the rowdiest the capital city had ever seen. Crowds pushed through a barrier on the White House steps and joined the official celebration, guzzling punch, gobbling ice cream, and standing on the furniture to get a better look at their hero. Senator Daniel Webster glumly noted that "they [the people] seem to think the country is rescued from some dreadful danger."

This pro-Jackson cartoon (right) from the election of 1824 shows Jackson—in his general's uniform—surrounded by a snarling pack of political "curs" (mongrel dogs). The "curs" represent Jackson's opponents in the election and the newspaper editors who supported them. Although Jackson won the most popular votes in the election, the House of Representatives finally declared John Quincy Adams the winner.

"President's Levee or All Creation Going to the White House" is the title of this aquatint (below) by Robert Cruikshank. It shows a crowd of Washingtonians arriving at the White House to attend Jackson's inauguration. Because Rachel Robards Jackson died shortly after her husband's election, Emily Donelson, wife of Jackson's adopted son, served as official hostess at the White House during most of the time Jackson was in office.

President Jackson lived in constant pain. He suffered from several diseases, including tuberculosis, and he carried three bullets in his body—grisly souvenirs of his days as a brawling, dueling young frontiersman. When one bullet was removed from his arm in 1832, Jackson gave it to the man who had put it there—former enemy Thomas Hart Benton, who later became Jackson's friend. "I had a fight with Jackson," Benton said later. "A fellow was hardly in fashion who didn't."

A STORMY ADMINISTRATION

President Jackson came into office publicly proclaiming the authority of the common man. "The majority is to govern," he stated in his first annual message to Congress in 1829. However, once in office, he fired many government employees and replaced them with his friends and supporters. Some politicians complained about this favoritism, but Jackson felt, in the words of Senator William Marcy, that "to the victor belongs the spoils [rewards]." And instead of going to his regular cabinet for advice, President Jackson chose to meet with a group of trusted friends. Because this group met in the White House kitchen, Jackson's critics dubbed it the "Kitchen Cabinet." Before long, Jackson was at odds with his official cabinet and his vice president, the brilliant, ambitious John C. Calhoun of South Carolina. By the election of 1832, most of the original cabinet members had resigned or been replaced.

Jackson also tangled with the Bank of the United States, which handled federal funds. In the summer of 1832, the bank's president, Nicholas Biddle, asked Congress to renew its charter (federal authorization). Congress did so, but President Jackson vetoed the bill. He believed the bank served only "to make the rich richer and the potent more powerful" at the expense of workers and farmers. Despite Biddle's attempt to manipulate the nation's economy into a depression, Jackson refused to back down. The "Monster," as Jackson called the bank, was dead.

In 1834, the Senate adopted a resolution censuring (reprimanding) President Jackson for his actions against the bank. After the heated "Bank War" cooled down, however, some senators regretted the action—including Thomas Hart Benton of Missouri. He launched an effort to expunge (remove) the censure resolution from the Senate records. This cartoon (opposite, top) mocks Benton by portraying him as a spider rolling a huge ball single-mindedly toward the Capitol. In 1837, however, Benton's effort succeeded and the resolution was removed.

"You are a den of vipers and thieves," said Jackson of the Bank of the United States. "I intend to rout you out, and by the Eternal God, I will rout you out!" This cartoon (right) shows the president waving his order for the removal of government money from the bank while terrified bank officials flee. The figure to the right of Jackson is Major Jack Downing, a popular fictional character of the era who often appeared in political cartoons. Like many political cartoons at this time, this print uses language that would be considered racist and offensive today.

In this cartoon (above), Nicholas Biddle, president of the Bank of the United States, squares off with President Jackson (right, with glasses) in a frontier-style bare-knuckle boxing match. In 1834, a group of Baltimore businessmen tried to persuade Jackson that his war with the bank was crippling the nation's economy and hurting "the people." Furious, Jackson rose to his feet and shouted, "The people, sir, are with me!"

In 1828, the state of Georgia tried to seize millions of acres of land belonging to the Cherokee Indians. The Supreme Court, led by Chief Justice John Marshall, upheld the Cherokees' claim to their homeland in 1832. Jackson, however, defied the court and ordered the army to remove the Cherokees, reportedly saying, "John Marshall has made his decision—now let him enforce it!" The Cherokees were forced to move to Indian Territory (now Oklahoma), the area shown on this 1836 map (opposite, top).

Andrew Jackson survived the first presidential assassination attempt. On January 30, 1835, Jackson was leaving a funeral service in the Capitol building when Richard Lawrence fired two pistols at him from a distance of six feet, as depicted in this illustration (right). Both guns misfired, and Jackson was uninjured. Lawrence, an unemployed housepainter, was declared insane three months later and sent to an asylum for life.

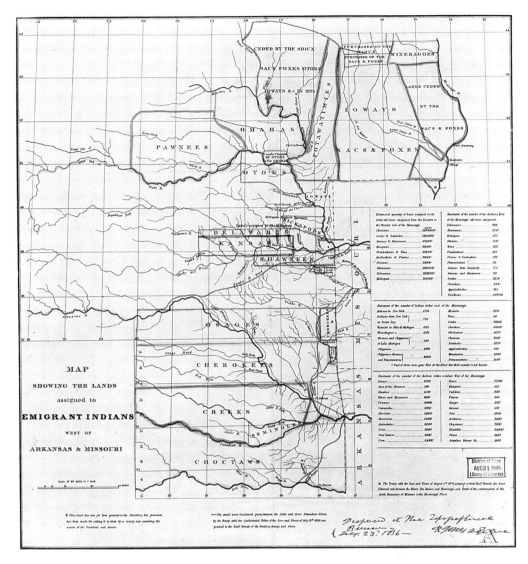

JACKSON'S LATER YEARS

The election of 1832 pitted Jackson against Senator Henry Clay of Kentucky, candidate of the National-Republican Party. Jackson was the winner, and Martin Van Buren of New York was elected vice president, replacing John C. Calhoun, who had resigned to take a seat in the Senate from South Carolina.

In the midst of the election, a major crisis shook the Jackson administration. In 1828, Congress had passed a tariff on manufactured goods imported from Europe. This tariff helped Northern factories sell their products, but it hurt planters in the South. South Carolina officials, led by Calhoun, boldly declared that states had the right to nullify (declare invalid) federal laws they believed to be unconstitutional—including the tariff. For a time, it seemed as if South Carolina would secede from the Union. Jackson, however, acted quickly and forcefully, even threatening to use troops against South Carolina, and the crisis passed.

Worn down by his stormy eight years in office, Jackson did not seek a third term. He had the satisfaction of seeing Martin Van Buren, his chosen successor, win the election of 1836. In 1837, Jackson retired to the Hermitage, although he remained an influential leader in the Democratic Party. On June 8, 1845, the veteran of so many military and political battles died peacefully in his bed.

This Currier & Ives lithograph (right) shows Andrew Jackson's death on June 8, 1845. Jackson died surrounded by his family and many of his slaves. His last words were "I hope to see you all in Heaven, both white and black, both white and black." Jackson was buried alongside his beloved wife in the Hermitage's garden.

By the time Jackson left the White House in 1837, the Hermitage included nearly a thousand acres of land and a magnificent mansion, as depicted in this lithograph (below). The mansion replaced a brick house that had burned down in 1834. In the eight years between the end of Jackson's presidency and his death, Democratic Party leaders often traveled to the Hermitage to seek the ex-president's advice.

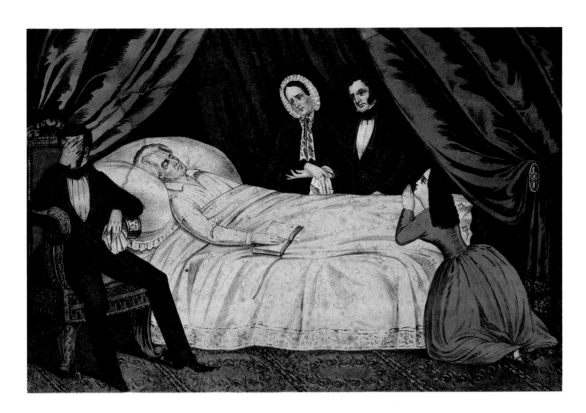

MARTIN VAN BUREN: "OLD KINDERHOOK"

Martin Van Buren was born in Kinderhook, New York, on December 5, 1782.
His hometown's name later became
one of his nicknames. A descendant of
Dutch settlers in New York's Hudson
Valley, Van Buren grew up in near
poverty. After receiving some formal
schooling, he began studying law in
1796. He began a successful law practice at Kinderhook in 1803, and four
years later married Hannah Hoess.
The couple had four children before
Hannah's death in 1819. Van Buren
never remarried.

In 1812, Van Buren entered politics
as a state senator. Quick-witted and
likable, he eventually became the head
of New York's "Albany Regency," a
powerful group in what would become
the Democratic Party. Elected to the
U.S. Senate in 1821, he allied himself
with Andrew Jackson. Van Buren was
elected governor of New York in 1829,
but he resigned after only two months
in office when Jackson offered him the
post of secretary of state.

Van Buren proved invaluable to
Jackson. When Van Buren resigned
his cabinet post in 1831, he shamed
many of the others into resigning as
well. Jackson made him U.S. minister
to Great Britain, but Vice President
John C. Calhoun blocked the appointment (using his authority as leader of
the Senate). Furious at Calhoun, Jackson replaced him with Van Buren for
the vice presidency in 1832.

Little is known about Hannah Hoess Van Buren (1783–1819; left), who died eighteen years before Martin Van Buren became president. (Van Buren's daughter-in-law, Angelica Singleton, served as hostess during his presidency.) When Hannah died at the age of thirty-six, an Albany newspaper wrote: "Modest and unassuming, possessing the most engaging simplicity of manners, her heart was the residence of every kind of affection, and glowed with sympathy for the wants and sufferings of others."

As President Jackson's secretary of state, Van Buren became embroiled in the Eaton Affair, a social scandal that wrecked Jackson's cabinet. It began when Secretary of War John Eaton married a young woman named Peggy O'Neil. Because of her questionable past, the wives of the other cabinet members refused to socialize with her. Jackson, a friend of the Eatons', angrily halted cabinet meetings until the cabinet wives stopped snubbing Peggy Eaton. Eventually, Van Buren ended the crisis by resigning in 1831. His action led the other members to quit, allowing the president to reorganize the cabinet. This anti-Eaton cartoon (below) depicts Peggy Eaton as a ballerina performing before the president.

"THE LITTLE MAGICIAN"

As Andrew Jackson's vice president and right-hand man, Van Buren easily won the Democratic nomination for the presidency in 1836. He faced opposition from a new political party, the Whigs, which had formed in 1834. Taking its name from the eighteenth-century English party that opposed King George III, the Whigs sought to limit the power of Andrew Jackson, whom they called "King Andy I." But the party was new and disorganized. In the 1836 elections, the Whigs ran no fewer than three candidates against Van Buren: Hugh White of Tennessee, William Henry Harrison of Indiana, and Daniel Webster of Massachusetts. Van Buren won with about 51 percent of the vote, while Whig support was split among the three challengers. He took office pledging to "tread generally in the footsteps of President Jackson."

The five-foot-six-inch Van Buren earned the nickname "the Little Magician" for his shrewdness and political skill. Right away he was faced with a crisis, as the Panic (financial depression) of 1837 began just after he took office. By the end of the year, as many as 90 percent of the factories on the East Coast had shut down. Falling crop prices spread the misery to the countryside. Van Buren proposed a plan for recovery that September, but it wasn't enough. The hard times continued throughout his administration.

Van Buren won in 1836, but it was a close shave for his controversial running mate, Richard Mentor Johnson (above). Although Johnson was famous for killing the great Indian leader Tecumseh (a claim many still dispute), he lived with an African-American woman, an arrangement many voters couldn't accept. At that time, voters still cast separate ballots for presidential and vice presidential candidates, and Johnson failed to win a majority. He was finally elected by the mostly Democratic Senate— the only such election in U.S. history.

"It will kill him, sir, kill him dead. He will never kick!" said Vice President John C. Calhoun, after he had successfully blocked Van Buren's nomination as U.S. minister to Great Britain. The ambitious Calhoun thought he had gotten rid of Van Buren as a political rival forever. A year later, however, Van Buren replaced Calhoun as vice president. In 1837, Calhoun had to watch as Van Buren was sworn in as president, a scene depicted in this woodcut (right).

Martin Van Buren (right) was a fifty-four-year-old widower when he took office in 1837. Many people assumed the sophisticated Van Buren would live elegantly as president. But one visitor to the White House—Dolley Madison, widow of president James Madison—found the atmosphere dull and dreary. Determined to make the White House more comfortable, she introduced her young cousin, Angelica Singleton, to Abraham Van Buren, the president's son and secretary. The two were married in 1838. Mrs. Madison's matchmaking gave the president an official hostess, who soon turned the White House into a festive place.

VAN BUREN'S LATER YEARS

Van Buren still had the support of the Democrats as the election of 1840 approached. By now, however, the Whigs were united and well organized. They adopted a favorite strategy of the Democrats: choosing a military hero, William Henry Harrison, as their candidate. After a riotous campaign that focused on personalities instead of issues, Harrison won the election.

Van Buren's political career was not over. He almost won the Democratic nomination in 1844, but lost because of his stand on Texas.

In 1836, American settlers in the Mexican province of Texas won their independence from Mexico. While many Americans hoped Texas would be annexed to the United States, others feared that admitting Texas as a slave state would upset the political balance between North and South. As the election approached, Van Buren and his most likely opponent, Henry Clay, both announced their opposition to annexation. Andrew Jackson, who supported annexation, felt that Van Buren had betrayed the Democratic Party by agreeing with Clay. The former president refused to support his old friend, and the nomination went to James K. Polk.

In 1848, Van Buren again ran unsuccessfully for president, this time as candidate of the antislavery Free Soil Party. He spent the remainder of his life quietly at Lindenwald, his New York estate. On July 24, 1862, Van Buren died, aged seventy-nine.

This is a "Grand Democratic Free Soil Banner" (above), which portrays the party's candidates in 1848—Van Buren and Charles Francis Adams, the son of John Quincy Adams. Van Buren wasn't the unanimous choice at the convention. One speaker, trying to show that the elderly ex-president still had energy, told how Van Buren had jumped over a fence to show a visitor his turnip patch. "Damn his turnips!" shouted a free soiler in the audience. "What are his opinions about the abolition of slavery in the District of Columbia?"

This political cartoon (right) from the election of 1848 depicts Van Buren as "The Modern Colossus." Van Buren was the candidate of the Free Soil Party, an uneasy alliance between antislavery Democrats from New York and antislavery members of other parties. Van Buren is seen trying to unite both sides of the new party. The cartoonist thinks he is about to fall into "Salt River"—nineteenth-century slang for political defeat. In fact, Van Buren won no electoral votes and only about 11 percent of the popular vote.

Titled "All the West going for Matty," this Whig cartoon (above) from 1840 shows the president (who hoped for the support of the Western states and territories) being pursued by wild animals from the Mississippi River and the "Alleghany" Mountains. "Matty" and "Matty Van" were two of Van Buren's many nicknames.

WILLIAM HENRY HARRISON

William Henry Harrison was born into a distinguished family in Charles City County, Virginia, on February 9, 1773. His father, Benjamin Harrison, was a signer of the Declaration of Independence who later served as governor of Virginia.

After attending Hampden-Sydney College, Harrison moved to Philadelphia to study medicine under Dr. Benjamin Rush, one of the young nation's greatest scientists. In 1791, Harrison left this field for the army. Commissioned as an ensign (junior officer) at the age of eighteen, he fought in many battles against Indians in the Northwest Territory (an area that later became the states of Indiana, Illinois, Ohio, Michigan, and Wisconsin). In 1795, Harrison married Anna Symmes and bought land near present-day North Bend, Ohio. He left the army in 1798 as a captain, and settled down in North Bend, expanding his original home—a log cabin—into a mansion.

In 1800, President John Adams appointed Harrison as the first governor of the Indiana Territory, where he served for thirteen years. Unlike many frontier politicians, Harrison proved both honest and capable. Governing the territory (which was much larger than the present-day state of Indiana) was a tough job, especially when it came to persuading the region's Indians to leave their homeland to make room for white settlers.

New Jersey-born Anna Symmes Harrison (1775–1864; right) had an exciting adventure as a small child during the Revolutionary War. Deciding she would be safer with relatives on Long Island, her father (a colonel in the Continental Army) disguised himself as a British officer to get four-year-old Anna through the enemy lines. Devoutly religious and devoted to her husband, Anna always hoped (in vain) that he would give up soldiering and politics. When he was elected president, she said sadly, "I wish my husband's friends had left him where he is, happy and contented in retirement."

North Bend, Ohio, was Harrison's home for most of his life. In 1795, he and Anna Harrison began their married life in a five-room log cabin at North Bend. Over the years the home was expanded into a sixteen-room house with fine furniture and woodwork. This engraving (below) shows how Harrison's home appeared about the time he ran for president.

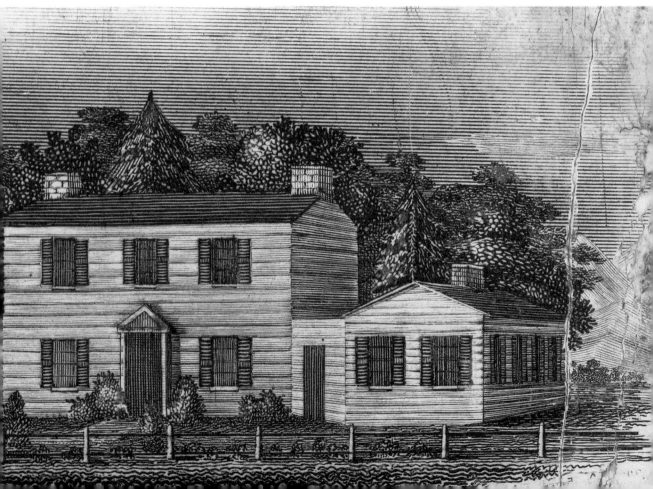

"OLD TIPPECANOE"

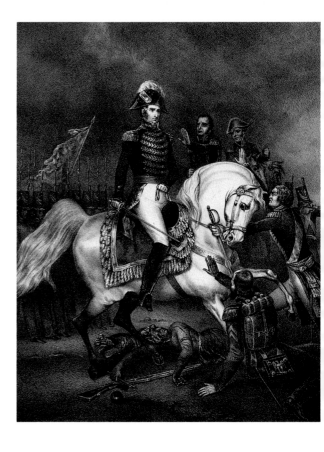

In 1811, President Madison ordered William Henry Harrison to take troops into an area in the Northwest claimed by both the Shawnee Indians and the government. On November 7, 1811, Indians attacked Harrison's troops along the banks of the Tippecanoe River. Harrison's volunteers fought off the attack, and, as a result, Harrison became a national hero.

During the War of 1812, Harrison was given the job of defending American territory along the Northwest frontier. On October 5, 1813, Harrison defeated a British and Indian force near the Thames River in Canada. Among the dead was Tecumseh, the Shawnee leader.

After the war, Harrison briefly retired to North Bend before going into politics. He served in the House, as an Ohio state senator, as a U.S. senator, and as U.S. minister to Colombia. In 1836, the new Whig Party, well aware of Harrison's fame as a war hero, selected him as one of its presidential candidates. Harrison lost to Martin Van Buren, but he was back for another try in 1840.

This fanciful lithograph (above) shows Harrison, in full uniform and mounted on a magnificent horse, at the Battle of Tippecanoe. In fact, when the shooting began, Harrison jumped on another officer's horse in the confusion of battle. The officer then mounted Harrison's horse and rode toward the fighting. Almost immediately, he was killed by Indian sharpshooters who, trained to recognize Harrison's horse, thought they were firing at the American commander.

With about 900 men under his command—some regular army troops, some volunteers—William Henry Harrison advanced into the northern part of the Indiana Territory in the autumn of 1811. On the banks of the Wabash River, near present-day Terre Haute, Harrison's troops built a log fort they named for their commander. This print (right) shows how Fort Harrison appeared about a year later.

"A Political Movement" is the title of this cartoon (above), which depicts a depressed, defeated Martin Van Buren leaving Washington in a wagon pulled by his political allies. The new president, William Henry Harrison, stands on the steps at right. Beside Harrison is the prominent Whig senator Henry Clay, who holds an eviction notice and a key to the White House.

Harrison's greatest military triumph came at the Battle of the Thames in October 1813. Before the battle, Tecumseh told his warriors, "We are about to enter an engagement from which I shall not return," and, indeed, he died in the fighting. Many credited Richard Mentor Johnson, leader of 1,000 Kentucky volunteers, with the death of Tecumseh, as shown in this print (below). The exact circumstances of the great Shawnee leader's death are unknown.

Ironically, it was the Democrats who gave the Whigs the theme for William Henry Harrison's famous—and successful—campaign of 1840. To promote the idea that he was too old and tired to be president, a Democratic supporter reported that someone had said of Harrison, "Give him a barrel of hard cider and a pension of about $2,000 a year and . . . he will sit the remainder of his days in a log cabin." The Whigs took this charge and flung it back at the Democrats by portraying "Old Tippecanoe" as a rough-hewn Westerner with simple tastes. This Whig campaign poster (above) shows Harrison greeting a maimed veteran. During the campaign, the Whigs gave out many souvenirs that related to the log-cabin-and-cider theme.

Shown here is a handkerchief with a portrait of Harrison—one of the countless mementos from the campaign of 1840. After Harrison's victory, Democrats sadly noted that the Whigs had won using strategies the Democrats had pioneered. "They have at last learned from defeat the art of victory," wrote one prominent Democrat. "We have taught them how to conquer us!"

A BRIEF PRESIDENCY

More Americans voted in the 1840 elections than ever before. Harrison won the presidency by a comfortable majority. His vice president was John Tyler, a former senator from Virginia.

Harrison was looking forward to his new position and expected to do great things at the White House. Daniel Webster had prepared a speech for Harrison's inauguration, thinking the new president would be too busy to write it. But Harrison insisted on doing the work himself, telling Webster, "If I should read your inaugural address instead of mine, everyone would know that you wrote it, and I did not." Webster offered to review the text and found that it was much too long, dwelling more on Roman history than on current American issues.

Harrison's inaugural on March 4, 1841, took place on a cold, wet day. His speech took nearly two hours to read, in spite of Webster's editing. Harrison, who refused to wear a coat at the ceremony, caught a cold. It turned into pneumonia. On April 4, exactly one month after taking office, Harrison became the first president to die while in office.

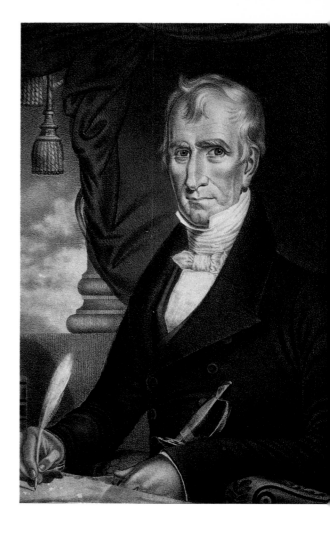

This lithograph (above) shows Harrison about the time he took office. At sixty-eight, he was at that time the oldest person to win the presidency. While that record has since been broken, Harrison still holds the record for the longest inaugural address—8,500 words, lasting two hours.

Ten thousand people attended William Henry Harrison's funeral procession. After ceremonies at the White House, the president was buried in a Washington cemetery. Eventually, however, the body was moved to a tomb (below) on the grounds of Harrison's estate at North Bend. Anna Harrison (who missed her husband's inaugural and never lived in the White House) lived for twenty-two years after Harrison's death. Among their ten children was John Scott Harrison (1804–30), father of Benjamin Harrison, who was elected president in 1888.

JOHN TYLER

John Tyler was born in Charles City County, Virginia, on March 29, 1790, not far from William Henry Harrison's birthplace. Tyler's father served as governor of Virginia, as did Harrison's.

Tyler's career got off to a quick start. A graduate of William and Mary at seventeen, he began practicing law at nineteen and was elected to the Virginia legislature at twenty-one. After brief service in the War of 1812, he married Letitia Christian. From 1817 to 1821, he represented Virginia in the House. He served as governor of the state from 1825 to 1827 and then as one of its U.S. senators.

In the Senate, Tyler won a reputation for being politically independent and unwilling to compromise his principles. Tyler's stubbornness led to a setback for him in 1836. Although he originally supported Andrew Jackson and agreed with many of his policies, Tyler voted to censure (reprimand) the president for removing federal money from the Bank of the United States. Later, the Virginia legislature told Tyler to vote for removing the censure resolution from the record. Tyler refused. At this time, state legislatures elected U.S. senators, so Tyler's stand cost him his Senate seat.

In 1840, Tyler accepted the Whig Party's vice presidential nomination. On April 6, 1841, two days after Harrison's death, Tyler was sworn in as president.

Tyler's marriage to his first wife, Letitia Christian Tyler (1790–1842; above), lasted twenty-nine years and produced eight children. During their five-year courtship, Tyler wrote poems to her and serenaded her on the violin. A quiet, religious woman, Letitia Tyler suffered a stroke two years before her husband became president. During her year and a half as First Lady, she was able to make only one public appearance.

Like many sons of aristocratic Virginia families, John Tyler attended the College of William and Mary (right). Founded in 1693, the college was the alma mater of two other presidents—Thomas Jefferson and James Monroe. Tyler graduated from William and Mary in 1807.

This portrait shows how John Tyler looked at twenty years of age. As a young attorney, he often made his rounds mounted on his horse, "the General." When his faithful horse died, Tyler buried him on the grounds of his home, under a tombstone with this inscription: "Here lies the body of my good horse, the General. For twenty years he bore me around the circuit of my practice, and in all that time he never made a blunder. Would that his master could say the same!"

TO THE CONFEDERACY

Many people felt Tyler had no right to the presidency. He gained a mocking nickname: "His Accidency." Some called for his resignation and a special election. But Tyler refused to consider himself "acting president," and Congress passed a resolution confirming his right to the White House.

Tyler's single term was stormy. He vetoed Whig-sponsored legislation and was then thrown out of the party. Most of his cabinet resigned. There was even an attempt to impeach him. The death of Letitia Tyler in 1842 added to his misfortunes. In February 1844, Tyler himself was nearly killed in an accident aboard an experimental warship.

A president without a party, Tyler knew he had no chance of reelection in 1844, so he took a controversial step. He negotiated an annexation treaty with the Republic of Texas, although he knew this move might mean war with Mexico, which had never truly accepted the loss of Texas. Soon after pro-annexation Democrat James K. Polk won the election, Congress passed a resolution to annex Texas. Tyler signed the measure just before leaving office.

Tyler thus helped set the stage for the Mexican War, which in turn put the nation on the road to the Civil War. When that conflict came, Tyler was elected to the Confederate Congress from Virginia. He died in 1862 before taking his seat.

Tyler's second wife was Julia Gardiner (above), daughter of New York senator David Gardiner. Despite a thirty-year age difference, Tyler and Julia fell in love and were married in New York City on June 26, 1844. They had seven children, the last when Tyler was seventy years old.

On February 28, 1844, President Tyler went for a cruise down the Potomac River aboard the USS Princeton, *the Navy's first propeller-driven steam warship. Tyler had just gone below decks to listen to a song when the* Princeton's *crew began test-firing one of its huge cannons. The weapon blew up, as depicted in this lithograph (opposite, top), killing six people and wounding nineteen others. The president would almost certainly have been one of the casualties if he had been on deck at the time.*

After leaving office, Tyler lived at Sherwood Forest, his plantation on the banks of the James River in Virginia. Although he participated in a failed "peace conference" between South and North early in 1861, Tyler supported secession and eagerly accepted a seat in the Confederate Congress.

Part II

The Coming Crisis

Three future presidents fought in the Battle of Monterrey during the Mexican War: Zachary Taylor and Ulysses S. Grant, who went on to become presidents of the United States, and Jefferson Davis, who would become president of the Confederate States of America in 1861. This lithograph shows American troops assaulting the high ground around the city.

The years between 1848 and 1861 were a time when the presidency failed as an institution. The presidents of those years did not meet the challenges before them. This, combined with other factors, led the United States into a crisis that threatened its very survival as a nation. The gap between North and South widened as the controversy over slavery (especially its spread to the new territories of the West) grew increasingly bitter. In response, existing political parties died or reorganized and new ones arose. Finally, the nation split in two and teetered on the brink of civil war.

In 1848, the presidency went to Whig candidate Zachary Taylor, a victorious commander of the Mexican War. Taylor died in July 1850 and was succeeded by Vice President Millard Fillmore. Fillmore and the two Democratic presidents who followed him, Franklin Pierce and James Buchanan, are sometimes called the "Doughface presidents." (The term "Doughface" meant a Northerner who would cave in, like dough, under the pressure of Southern influence.) The three tried to hold the country together by supporting half-measures and compromises, but none proved successful.

In 1854 a new party, the Republicans, formed to fight the extension of slavery. In 1860, its candidate, Abraham Lincoln, emerged as the winner in a four-way election. With Lincoln's victory, the gathering storm finally broke, as Southern states, led by South Carolina, began to secede from the Union.

JAMES K. POLK: EARLY YEARS

James Knox Polk was born in Meck-lenburg County, North Carolina, on November 2, 1795. When he was ten years old, Polk and his family walked from North Carolina to Tennessee, where they settled near Nashville. Polk's father established one of the biggest plantations in Tennessee, which Polk eventually inherited.

Polk returned to his home state to attend North Carolina University. After graduating in 1818, he studied law under a friend of Andrew Jacksons', beginning a long association with Old Hickory and the Democratic Party. In 1823, Polk was elected to the Ten-nessee legislature. The following year he married Sarah Childress, the daughter of a wealthy Tennessee planter.

In 1825, Polk began a fourteen-year stretch in the House of Representa-tives. Hardworking, resolute, and a firm supporter of President Jackson, Polk swiftly became an influential con-gressman. He served on the House Ways and Means Committee, became the Democratic majority leader, and, in 1835, was elected House Speaker. Polk held that post until 1839, when he successfully ran for governor of Ten-nessee. He lost two bids for reelection, however, and it seemed that his politi-cal career was over—until 1844, when the Democratic Party couldn't settle on a presidential candidate.

This map (right) shows settlements in Ten-nessee in 1822, four years after Polk came to Nashville to study law. His decision to remain in Tennessee and enter the legal profession led him to become friends with Andrew Jackson. As a Tennessee congress-man during Jackson's administration, Polk was one of the president's strongest sup-porters. In 1839 Polk returned to Nashville to serve as Tennessee's governor.

Polk (right) was a hardworking and intelligent politician, but he lacked the dynamic personality needed to attract a large following. During his seven consecutive terms in the House of Representatives, he earned the nickname "Polk the Plodder." This portrait was drawn while Polk was governor of Tennessee (1839–41).

Sarah Childress Polk (1803–91; left) was born in Murfreesboro, Tennessee, to a wealthy plantation family. She received a complete formal education (unusual for women at that time), attending a girls' school in Nashville and a Protestant school for women in Salem, North Carolina.

Sarah Polk took a keen interest in politics—especially where her husband's career was concerned. James Polk once hinted that Sarah agreed to marry him only after he promised to run for Congress. "She is well read, has much talent for conversation, and is highly popular" was how one visitor to the White House described the First Lady. This manuscript (left) is the last page of one of Polk's letters to his wife regarding his private papers and letters.

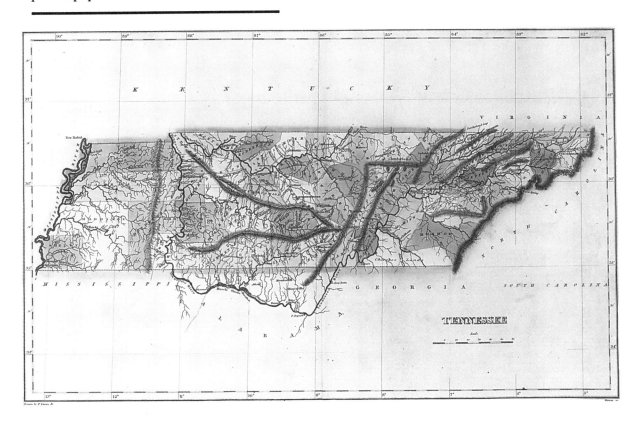

"THE DARK HORSE"

The Democrats couldn't agree on a candidate to run against Henry Clay, the Whig nominee. Martin Van Buren was out because he opposed the annexation of Texas, a stance that angered Andrew Jackson, still a powerful party leader. Polk's name first came up on the seventh ballot at the Democratic convention in Baltimore. On the ninth ballot, Polk won the presidential nomination.

James Knox Polk thus became the first "dark horse" presidential candidate. (A "dark horse" candidate is one who seems to come out of nowhere yet wins.) Despite his years as House Speaker, Polk was so little known nationwide that scornful Whigs began chanting "Who is James Polk?" at campaign rallies.

Candidate Polk called for "the reoccupation of Oregon and the reannexation of Texas." The Oregon Country—the region that now includes Washington State, Oregon, Idaho, and British Columbia—had been jointly ruled by the United States and Britain for years. But American settlers were now moving rapidly into Oregon, and many people wanted the United States to claim the entire region—even at the risk of war with Britain. The Texas question was even more controversial, because annexation of Texas meant another slave state in the Union, plus the likelihood of war with Mexico. But Polk's program convinced a slim majority of American voters, and he defeated Whig Henry Clay for the White House.

Polk's running mate in the election of 1844 was George Mifflin Dallas (1792–1864; above), a Philadelphia-born lawyer who had served as a senator from Pennsylvania and U.S. minister to Russia. Like Polk, Dallas was a strong supporter of annexation for Texas. When Texas entered the Union, grateful citizens named a county, and later a city, after him.

This Democratic campaign poster (opposite, top) celebrates Polk as "Young Hickory"—a successor to Andrew Jackson. Polk first met Jackson when the general was serving in the Tennessee legislature, and the older man did much to advance Polk's career. In turn, Polk loyally supported Jackson's policies after he was elected to Congress. Dallas is shown to his left.

The annexation of Texas—or the "Texas bombshell," as some called it—was one of the key issues in the election of 1844. The cartoon shown here (right) mocks Whig candidate Henry Clay (second from right), who began his campaign by opposing annexation, only to change his mind in an effort to win Southern votes.

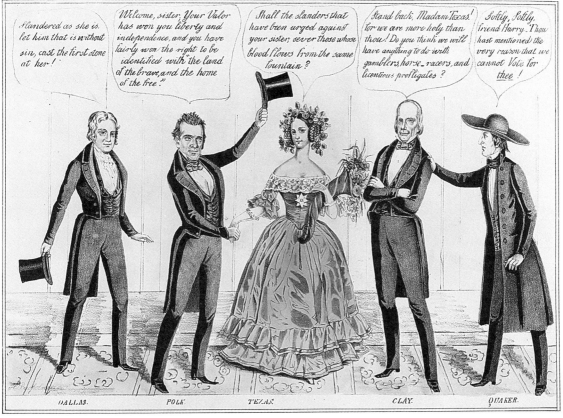

POLK AND MANIFEST DESTINY

During his campaign, Polk had promised not to run again in 1848 if he was elected in 1844. He took office in March 1845, determined to make the most of his single term.

Congress annexed Texas shortly before Polk took office, increasing tensions with Mexico. Perhaps for this reason, Polk settled the Oregon issue peacefully. In 1846, Polk persuaded Congress to accept a British proposal dividing Oregon into American and British territories at the 49th parallel.

Relations with Mexico, however, quickly worsened. Polk was a firm believer in "Manifest Destiny"—the idea that the United States had the right to expand across North America to the Pacific. To fulfill this goal, Polk wanted to add not only Texas but also California and New Mexico—both Mexican possessions at this time—to the United States.

In late 1845, Polk sent diplomat John Slidell to Mexico City with an offer to buy these territories. But the president was also prepared to fight. He ordered General Zachary Taylor at that same time to take an American army to an area of Texas that both Mexico and the U.S. claimed.

The Mexican government refused Slidell's offer. In April 1846, Mexican and U.S. troops clashed along the Rio Grande. Now Polk had what he most needed: an excuse to seize Mexican territory by force.

Diplomat John Slidell (1793–1871; right) was Polk's minister to the Mexican government. When he arrived in Mexico City in December 1845, however, the Mexican government refused even to listen to Polk's proposals to settle the dispute between the two nations. When an even more anti-American government came to power, in January 1846, Slidell was thrown out of Mexico. Born in New York but a Southerner by marriage, Slidell later served as a Confederate diplomat in Europe.

This 1846 view of an American settlement in Oregon (below) was painted by army officer Henry Warre. In the 1840s, many Americans wanted the United States to claim Oregon all the way up to latitude 54'40"— the southern border of present-day Alaska. This inspired the slogan "Fifty-four forty or fight!" The Oregon Country was home to only a handful of fur traders in the early 1800s, but the opening of the Oregon Trail in 1842 quickly brought thousands of settlers into the region.

THE MEXICAN WAR

On May 13, 1846, Congress passed a declaration of war against Mexico. In June 1846, a handful of American settlers in California, confident of Polk's support, declared independence from Mexico. In early 1847, a small army led by General Stephen Watts Kearny arrived to back them up. Along the way, Kearny put New Mexico under American rule.

In Mexico itself, however, U.S. forces had to overcome determined Mexican opposition. Zachary Taylor's army advanced into northern Mexico, winning major victories and finally halting after the Battle of Buena Vista in February 1847. In March, General Winfield Scott and 10,000 troops came ashore near the seaport of Veracruz. Scott then marched his forces into Mexico's interior, capturing Mexico City on September 14, 1847. In February 1848, U.S. and Mexican diplomats signed the Treaty of Guadalupe Hidalgo, ending the war. In return for about $18.5 million, Mexico agreed to give the United States more than 500,000 square miles of territory, including California and New Mexico.

President Polk had achieved all his goals, but the strain of running a wartime administration, along with ill health, took its toll. On June 15, 1849, just three months after leaving office, Polk died at his Tennessee plantation.

CALIFORNIA REPUBLIC

American settler William Todd designed this flag (above), featuring a red star and a grizzly bear, as a symbol for the short-lived "Bear Flag Republic" in California. The revolt against Mexican rule in California was encouraged by John C. Frémont, a U.S. Army officer. Frémont was supposedly leading an exploring expedition, but his real reason for being in California was probably to stir up trouble on orders from the Polk administration. Frémont later ran unsuccessfully as the Republican Party's first presidential candidate.

American forces advance on Chapultepec Castle, the fortress protecting Mexico City, in this Currier & Ives print (opposite, top). Among those present at the capture of the city was future president Ulysses S. Grant, then a young officer with Scott's army. In his memoirs, Grant called the Mexican War "one of the most unjust ever waged by a stronger against a weaker nation."

President Polk's health was never good, and he was very weak by the time he left office in March 1849. (Living conditions in the White House, which had no indoor plumbing at the time, may have contributed to Polk's illnesses.) The ex-president spent only three months in retirement at his Nashville home, "Polk Place," before his death. The mansion was destroyed in 1900, nine years after the death of Jane Polk, who survived her husband by forty-two years. This engraving (right) shows his tomb, located at the Polk Place estate.

ZACHARY TAYLOR: "OLD ROUGH AND READY"

Zachary Taylor was born in Orange County, Virginia, on November 24, 1784. As an infant, Taylor moved with his family to Kentucky. Growing up on what was then the frontier, young Zachary received a sketchy education from private tutors.

At the age of twenty-three, Taylor won a lieutenant's commission in the U.S. Army with the help of his cousin James Madison (then secretary of state). Although he later owned two plantations (and 150 slaves), Taylor's true home was the military until he arrived in the White House. In 1810, Taylor married Margaret Smith. She and their six children shared Taylor's hardships as a frontier officer.

Taylor served with distinction in the War of 1812, and then retired. In 1816, he was back in uniform again as a major. He led a regiment in the Black Hawk War in 1832 against Indians in Illinois and Wisconsin. In 1837, Taylor was ordered to Florida, where the army was fighting the Seminole Indians. Here Taylor earned the nickname "Old Rough and Ready," from his habit of wearing comfortable civilian clothes instead of a uniform. Despite his unmilitary appearance, Taylor soon won promotion to general and overall command in Florida. In 1845, President Polk picked Taylor to command the troops occupying the newly annexed territory of Texas.

For seven years, from 1835 to 1842, the Seminole Indians of Florida fiercely resisted attempts to remove them from their homeland. The battle depicted in this lithograph (above) took place at Lake Okeechobee on December 25, 1837. Zachary Taylor won promotion to brigadier general for his leadership in the fight.

Tents stretch to the sunbaked horizon in this print (right), which shows General Taylor's army camped near Corpus Christi, Texas, in the autumn of 1845. In the spring of 1846, Taylor moved his 3,000 soldiers to Fort Brown on the banks of the Rio Grande, just across from the Mexican town of Matamoros. Taylor's job was to maintain an American presence along Texas's disputed southern boundary.

BATTLES, MILITARY AND POLITICAL

In the spring of 1846, Zachary Taylor moved his "Army of Observation" into disputed territory between the Nueces River and the Rio Grande. After the fighting started, Taylor's troops marched south into Mexico, scoring victories at Resaca de la Palma and Palo Alto, capturing the city of Monterrey, and finally defeating a large Mexican force at Buena Vista.

Despite these victories, Taylor and President Polk were soon at odds. The president criticized some of Taylor's actions, such as declaring an eight-week truce after the capture of Monterrey. Finally, Polk ordered Taylor to halt his advance into Mexico. Polk had come to see Taylor, by now a popular hero, as a political rival. Although Polk didn't plan to run for reelection, he wanted to see a Democrat win the White House in 1848, and he feared the Whigs might nominate Taylor.

Polk was right. Early in 1848, a letter arrived at Taylor's headquarters. In those days, postage was paid by the addressee. Not recognizing the sender's name, the general refused to pay the postage. Only later did Taylor learn that the letter contained an offer of the Whig nomination for the presidency.

Taylor finally accepted the nomination. In the election, he defeated Democrat Lewis Cass and former president Martin Van Buren, now the candidate of the Free Soil Party.

"An Available Candidate" is the title of this cartoon (left), which shows Taylor atop a mountain of skulls. It pokes fun at the movement to make Taylor, a military hero, into a political leader. At first, Taylor ridiculed the idea of himself as president. "Stop your nonsense and drink your whiskey!" Taylor shouted when someone first proposed him as a candidate. But by the end of the war, Taylor—who had no political experience and had never even voted—decided the idea wasn't so ridiculous.

This lithograph (below), which is supposed to show Taylor at the Battle of Resaca de la Palma on May 9, 1846, is based more on imagination than fact. First, the artist shows Taylor in a slashing swordfight with a Mexican cavalryman—an incident that never happened. Second, Taylor is depicted in a fancy uniform. Actually, Taylor's casual attitude toward clothing was legendary. "Old Rough and Ready" was more likely to wear an old coat and a straw hat into battle than the full-dress uniform shown here.

THE SOLDIER-PRESIDENT

A crucial issue—the expansion of slavery—dominated Zachary Taylor's sixteen months as president. The Mexican War had added a huge chunk of land to the United States. Soon it would be organized into states and territories. But would these new states and territories allow slavery?

Taylor was a Southerner by birth, and a slaveowner. But his army career had given him a national outlook. At first, Taylor felt slavery should be kept out of the new lands. Later, he told Congress that the people of the new states and territories should decide the issue themselves. Unfortunately, events soon ruled out such a simple solution.

In 1848, gold was discovered in California. Many fortune seekers came to the area. As its population quickly grew, the territory asked for admission to the Union as a free (non-slave) state in 1849. Because this would upset the balance between free and slave states, Southern politicians opposed California's admission. As tensions mounted, some congressmen proposed a compromise. Taylor opposed this, believing it would only postpone, not solve, the problem.

At the height of the debate, Taylor attended an Independence Day ceremony at the unfinished Washington Monument. The sixty-five-year-old president fell ill after a day in the broiling sun, and on July 9, 1850, he died. Leadership of the nation fell to Taylor's vice president, Millard Fillmore.

Although this lithograph (opposite, top) shows President Taylor in full uniform, Taylor kept his casual style of dress even after moving into the White House. One visitor wrote that Taylor had "the least pretension . . . of any man I ever saw. It is remarkable that such a man should be president of the United States." To relax, Taylor galloped around the White House grounds on "Old Whitey," the cavalry horse that had carried him through Mexico.

After a hot July 4, 1850, Taylor drank a quantity of iced milk, ate several bowls of cherries and cucumbers, and went to bed with a stomachache. The illness turned into a fever, and a week later he was dead. Some historians believe that Taylor, still strong at sixty-five, might have survived if it hadn't been for the doctors who swarmed around his bedside, giving him one kind of useless medicine after another. This lithograph (right) shows Taylor's death on July 11. His last words were "I have always done my duty. I am ready to die. My only regret is for the friends I leave behind."

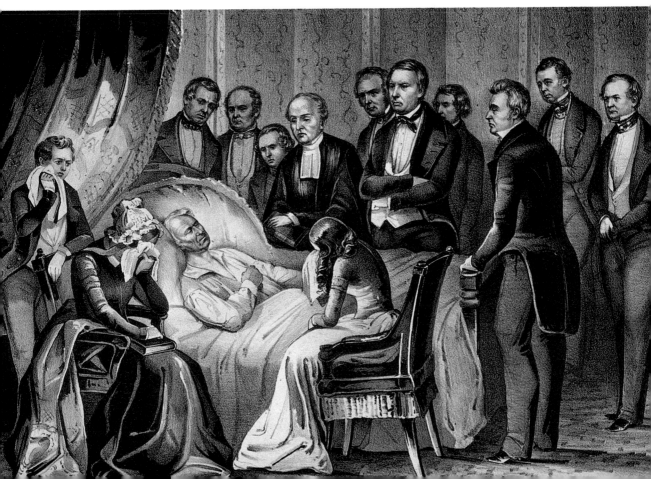

MILLARD FILLMORE: EARLY YEARS

Millard Fillmore was born on January 7, 1800, to a struggling farm family in Cayuga County, New York. One of nine children, Fillmore received little schooling. At fourteen, he was sent to learn the clothmaker's trade as an apprentice—an unpaid assistant. During this time, he was befriended by Abigail Powers, a young schoolteacher almost two years his senior. She gave him books to read and encouraged him to continue his education. Eventually, Fillmore saved up enough money to buy his way out of the hated apprenticeship arrangement.

Fillmore studied law as a clerk in the office of a local judge, beginning his own practice at age twenty-three. In 1826, he married Abigail Powers, and four years later the couple moved to Buffalo.

Fillmore got his start in politics by winning a seat in the New York legislature in 1828, a seat he kept until 1832. Fillmore's greatest accomplishment during this period was sponsoring a bill that protected debtors from prison. (In New York at the time, a person could be imprisoned if he or she was unable to repay loans.) In 1832, his supporters rewarded his hard work and ability by electing him to the House of Representatives.

Abigail Powers Fillmore (1799–1853; left) began her career as a schoolteacher at sixteen, and her love of learning continued throughout her life. As First Lady, she was shocked to discover that the White House had no library, and she urged her husband to ask Congress for the money to build one. By 1852, however, Abigail was in poor health, and she caught pneumonia during the inauguration of her husband's successor, Franklin Pierce. Just two weeks after leaving the White House, she died.

Millard Fillmore began his law studies as a clerk in the office of Judge Wood, a retired justice and "country lawyer" in Erie County, New York. In return for room, board, and legal training, Fillmore did chores around the judge's office. This woodcut (below), from an early biography of Fillmore, shows the young man's first meeting with Judge Wood.

FILLMORE TAKES OFFICE

Millard Fillmore served in the House for eleven years. He joined the new Whig Party and soon became one of its most influential Northern members. In 1844, he left Congress to run for the governorship of New York. Defeated by a slim margin, he was elected comptroller (chief financial officer) of the state in 1847.

In 1848, Fillmore won the Whig vice presidential nomination. The Whigs picked him to balance the ticket. Fillmore was an experienced politician, in sharp contrast to Zachary Taylor. Fillmore also helped win votes from Northern Whigs who felt uneasy about Taylor's Southern roots. In July 1850, Taylor's death brought Fillmore into the White House.

Fillmore took over the leadership of a nation in crisis. As vice president, Fillmore had disagreed with Taylor's response to the problems posed by California's request for statehood. Now, as president, Fillmore declared his support for the compromise measures proposed by Senator Henry Clay.

In December, Fillmore signed into law the bills known as the Compromise of 1850. They called for admitting California as a free state, but the slavery question in the territories of Utah and New Mexico was to be decided later. The Compromise also outlawed trading slaves in the District of Columbia, but added a strict federal fugitive slave law.

Unlike Zachary Taylor, Fillmore was careful about his appearance. Some people felt he needed to pay more attention to his job. "Fillmore is a great man," said one politician, "but it takes pressure to make him show his highest powers." This photograph (above), taken by the famous photographer Mathew Brady, shows Fillmore about the time he succeeded to the presidency.

A lavish parade (opposite, top) was held in San Francisco on October 29, 1850, to mark California's admission to the Union—a result of the Compromise of 1850. "God knows I detest slavery," said Fillmore before the compromise became law, "but it is an existing evil, for which we are not responsible, and we must endure it, and give it such protection as is guaranteed by the Constitution, till we can get rid of it without destroying the last hope of free government in the world."

The major foreign-policy achievement of Fillmore's administration was the "opening" of Japan, a nation that had been isolated from the world by its military rulers for over two centuries. In 1852, Fillmore sent a naval squadron under Commodore Matthew Perry to Japan with a message proposing a trade agreement. Perry arrived in Japan in July 1853, and in February 1854, American and Japanese representatives signed the treaty. A Japanese artist created this woodblock print (right) of one of Perry's warships at anchor off Edo (present-day Tokyo).

FILLMORE: LATER YEARS

The Compromise of 1850 postponed the split between North and South for a decade, but it destroyed the Whig Party and ruined Fillmore's chances for reelection. Even moderate Northern Whigs were angered by the Compromise's Fugitive Slave Law, which forced local authorities in the free states to help return escaped slaves to their masters.

It was a divided, dispirited Whig Party that met in Baltimore to pick a candidate for the election of 1852. After fifty-three ballots, the Whigs passed over Fillmore to nominate General Winfield Scott. For the first time, however, the Whig strategy of nominating a military hero failed. Democrat Franklin Pierce won the election. Fillmore tried to return to the White House in 1856, as the candidate of the American Party. This group, also called the "Know-Nothings," opposed immigration, Roman Catholicism, and anything else they felt was "un-American." On their ticket, Fillmore won fewer than a million votes.

Fillmore spent the rest of his days in Buffalo, where he was active in local affairs. During the Civil War, he supported the Union, although he disliked Abraham Lincoln. Fillmore died at the age of seventy-four on March 8, 1874.

After his unsuccessful bid for a return to the presidency on the Know-Nothing ticket, Fillmore became a civic leader in Buffalo. There, he helped found the University of Buffalo, the city Historical Society, and other institutions. After his death in 1874, Fillmore was buried in this tomb (above) in Buffalo's Forest Lawn Cemetery.

Former president Fillmore and his second wife, Caroline McIntosh (whom he married in 1858), lived in Buffalo, New York. Their house is shown is this engraving. After President Abraham Lincoln's assassination on April 15, 1865, an angry mob splashed red ink over the house. The vandals felt Fillmore was insulting the murdered president's memory by not immediately draping his home in mourning cloth.

FRANKLIN PIERCE

Franklin Pierce was born in Hillsboro, New Hampshire, on November 23, 1804. His father, a former army officer, served as a state legislator and later as governor of the state. Young Frank attended private schools and then, at the age of fifteen, entered Bowdoin College in Maine. There he met Nathaniel Hawthorne, who went on to become one of the nation's finest novelists. In 1852, Hawthorne would write Pierce's campaign biography.

Pierce came close to flunking out of Bowdoin. His friends convinced him to work harder, and in 1824 he graduated third in his class. After college, Pierce studied law and was elected to the New Hampshire state legislature in 1829. Four years later, Pierce won a seat in the House of Representatives, where he gained a reputation as a loyal Jackson Democrat. The following year, Pierce married Jane Appleton, daughter of a former Bowdoin College president.

In 1836, Pierce, at age thirty-two, became the nation's youngest senator. But his influence was limited in a Senate dominated by such political giants as Henry Clay and Daniel Webster. Also Jane Appleton Pierce hated Washington. In 1842, he resigned from the Senate and returned to his home in New Hampshire.

Novelist Nathaniel Hawthorne (1804–64; above), the author of The Scarlet Letter *and other classic works, was Pierce's Bowdoin College classmate and lifelong friend. When Pierce became president, he gave the struggling writer a job as U.S. consul in Liverpool, England. Hawthorne died while on a camping trip with Pierce in 1864.*

Franklin Pierce grew up in this house (below) located three miles from the town of Hillsboro, New Hampshire. "Pierce Homestead" was not only the home of the Pierce family but also the site of a tavern run by Pierce's father, Benjamin.

Jane Appleton Pierce (1806–63; right) was shy and religious. She disliked politics. When her husband was serving in the House, she confided to a friend: "Oh, how I wish he was out of political life! How much better it would be for him on every account!" The Pierces' son Benjamin died in a train accident shortly before Franklin Pierce's inauguration. As First Lady, Jane Pierce was too grief-stricken by the loss to appear at social functions.

Bowdoin College in Brunswick, Maine, played an important part in Pierce's life. It was here he met his friend and future campaign biographer Nathaniel Hawthorne. In 1834, ten years after graduating, Pierce married Jane Appleton, the daughter of Bowdoin's president. This print (below) shows the college's buildings and grounds in 1821.

"YOUNG HICKORY"

Franklin Pierce continued his law practice in Hillsboro and remained active in the Democratic Party. When the Mexican War broke out in 1846, Pierce enlisted in the army as a private, partly because of his loyalty to President Polk. Pierce was quickly promoted to colonel and finally to brigadier general. He was a dedicated officer. During the Battle of Contreras, Pierce was seriously injured when his horse fell on him, but he refused to leave the battlefield.

Pierce reentered national politics in 1852, when the Democratic Party was trying to select a presidential candidate. Senators Lewis Cass and Stephen Douglas were among the famous figures seeking the nomination. The party found these politicians too controversial and selected Pierce as a compromise. Franklin Pierce defeated Whig candidate Winfield Scott by a narrow majority in the popular vote but by a decisive margin in the Electoral College.

"Handsome Frank" Pierce (above) was tall and courtly in appearance, with a dark complexion and black hair. Forty-eight years old at the time of his inauguration, Pierce was the youngest president up to that time in U.S. history. He was also the first president to be born in the nineteenth century.

During the presidential campaign, the Whigs made much of the fact that Pierce had fainted twice in battle during the Mexican War. On one occasion, Pierce fainted from pain when his horse fell on him; on the second, he passed out from the heat. The Whigs exaggerated these incidents by portraying Pierce as a coward in political cartoons like this (right), which shows a queasy Pierce staying behind as his troops go into action. For their part, the Democrats attacked Whig candidate Winfield Scott, a lifelong soldier, as a "weak, conceited, foolish, blustering disciple of gunpowder."

A Democratic banner (right) from the election of 1852 shows Pierce and his running mate, Senator William King of Alabama. As they had done for James K. Polk, Democratic Party leaders tried to boost Pierce's popularity by linking him with Andrew Jackson. Campaign literature described Pierce as "Young Hickory of the Granite Hills" of New Hampshire—a fitting successor to "Old Hickory," Andrew Jackson.

KANSAS AND CONTROVERSY

The most significant event of Franklin Pierce's presidency was the passage of the Kansas-Nebraska Act. The bill, sponsored by Democratic senator Stephen Douglas, organized a stretch of Western land into the territories of Kansas and Nebraska. The issue of slavery in the new territories was to be decided by the settlers themselves—a process Douglas called "popular sovereignty."

Northerners opposed this bill, arguing that it would overturn the Missouri Compromise of 1820. The Compromise had outlawed slavery north of latitude 36'30", an area that included the new territories. Pierce strongly favored the bill, and with his backing it passed into law in May 1854. The result was anarchy and violence as pro- and anti-slavery settlers rushed into Kansas, each side trying to win a majority in the elections for the new territorial government.

Pierce's support for the bill cost him the support of many Northern Democrats. The party passed over him in 1856, nominating James Buchanan for president instead. After leaving office, Pierce returned to his New Hampshire law practice. Following his wife's death in 1863, Pierce fell into the grip of alcoholism. He spent his last years in loneliness and depression and died on October 8, 1869, at age sixty-four.

William King (1786–1853; above) was the only vice president to have been sworn in outside the United States. King, who suffered from tuberculosis, was trying to regain his health in Cuba when inauguration day arrived. An act of Congress let him take the oath of office "under the clear sky of the tropics" in Havana. King died a month later without returning to the United States, leaving the nation without a vice president until 1857.

One of the most dramatic confrontations of Pierce's presidency took place on May 22, 1856, on the Senate floor. On May 19, Massachusetts senator Charles Sumner made an angry speech against slavery. Part of the speech was directed against Senator Andrew Butler of South Carolina. Three days later, Representative Preston Brooks of South Carolina—a relative of Butler's—avenged the "insult" by beating Sumner into unconsciousness with a cane. This lithograph (opposite, top) by Winslow Homer shows the scene.

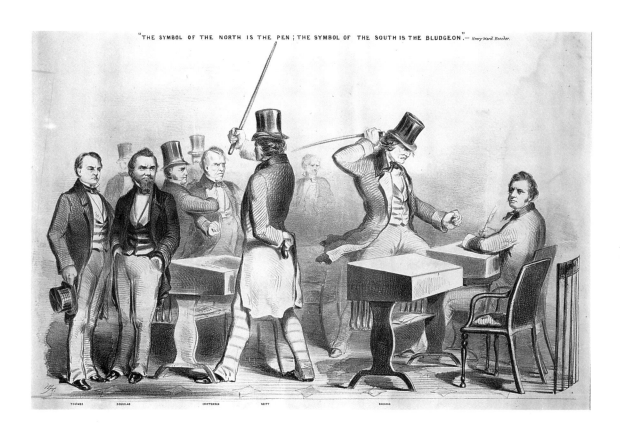
"THE SYMBOL OF THE NORTH IS THE PEN; THE SYMBOL OF THE SOUTH IS THE BLUDGEON."— *Henry Ward Beecher.*

"UNION IS STRENGTH."

FREE STATE CONVENTION!

All who are favorable to union

of effort, and a permanent organization of all those who desire to make Kansas a Free State, and who wish to secure, upon the broadest platform, the co-operation of all who agree upon this point, are requested to meet in their respective districts, and appoint Delegates who shall meet in general Convention at

BIG SPRING, THIRD DISTRICT,

On Wednesday, September 5th,

For the purpose of adopting a Platform upon which all may act harmoniously who prefer Freedom to Slavery.

The nomination of a Delegate to Congress, will also come up before the General Convention.

Every District will be entitled to five Delegates for each Representative apportioned by the Governor previously to the last election.

Let no sectional or party issues distract or prevent the perfect co-operation of Free State men. Union and harmony are absolutely necessary to success. The pro-slavery party are fully and effectually organized. No jars nor minor issues divide them. And to contend against them successfully, we also must be united. Without prudence and harmony of action we are certain to fail.

Let every man then do his duty and we are certain of victory.

All Free State men, without distinction, are earnestly requested to take immediate and effective steps to insure a full and correct representation for every District in the Territory.

The Delegates to represent the First and Second Districts in the Convention, will be chosen on the occasion of the

Mass Meeting

To be held at Lawrence on August 14th. The residents of these Districts are requested to attend this meeting.

"United we stand; divided we fall."

By order of the meeting held at Lawrence, July 17, 1855.

["Kansas Free State" Print.]

"I believe that involuntary servitude [slavery] . . . is recognized by the Constitution. I believe that it stands like any other admitted right," said Pierce in his inaugural address. He put this belief into action by backing the Kansas-Nebraska Act of 1854, a law that turned the territory into a battleground between antislavery "free soilers" and proslavery "border ruffians." This 1855 broadside announces a meeting of free soil settlers.

JAMES BUCHANAN: EARLY YEARS

James Buchanan was born in a log cabin in Mercersburg, Pennsylvania, on April 23, 1791. The oldest of eleven children, young Buchanan helped his Scotch-Irish immigrant father build a small country store into a prosperous business. Like Franklin Pierce, Buchanan was a high-spirited young man who didn't like to study. He was expelled from Dickinson College as a freshman, but he was allowed back the following year and graduated first in his class in 1809. Law study followed, and in 1813 Buchanan established his own practice in Lancaster, Pennsylvania. A year later, Buchanan enlisted in the U.S. Army during the War of 1812.

Returning to Pennsylvania, James Buchanan served in the state legislature, from 1814 to 1816. He then returned to his law practice and became engaged to Ann Coleman, the daughter of a Lancaster factory owner. She broke off the engagement, apparently because her parents disliked Buchanan. When she died a short time later, Buchanan wrote, "I feel that happiness has fled from me forever." He never married.

Buchanan entered national politics by winning a seat in the House of Representatives in 1820. He became a supporter of Andrew Jackson, and in 1828 joined the Democratic Party. In 1831, Jackson rewarded Buchanan's loyalty with an appointment as U.S. minister to Russia.

When James Buchanan became U.S. minister to Russia in 1832, that nation occupied Alaska and maintained fur-trading posts in what is now California. This print (above) shows the Russian fort at Bodega Bay near what is now San Francisco, about 1828. By the end of Buchanan's long life, Russia had given up its claims on the Pacific Coast and sold Alaska to the United States.

Although he was born in this modest log cabin (right), James Buchanan and his family escaped the hardships of the frontier. As a boy, "Jimmie" Buchanan helped his storekeeper father as a bookkeeper; for the rest of his life, Buchanan kept careful records of his income and expenses. Once, he refused to cash a check for $15,000 because the amount was wrong by 10 cents.

JAMES BUCHANAN
BORN APRIL 23 1791
PASSED HIS SCHOOLBOY DAYS IN MERCERSBURG
BECAME A LAWYER, MEMBER OF THE LEGISLATURE AND
OF CONGRESS, MINISTER TO RUSSIA, MEMBER OF THE
UNITED STATES SENATE, SECRETARY OF STATE,
MINISTER TO GREAT BRITAIN AND THE FIFTEENTH
PRESIDENT OF THE UNITED STATES
HIS PERSONAL INTEGRITY AND HONORABLE
CAREER ARE WORTHY OF EMULATION BY ALL TRUE
AMERICANS

DIPLOMAT AND PRESIDENT

James Buchanan spent two years at the Russian capital, St. Petersburg, before returning home in 1834 to take up a Senate seat. He remained in the Senate for eleven years. Buchanan strongly supported James Polk in the election of 1844, and in 1845 Polk appointed Buchanan secretary of state. After unsuccessfully seeking the Democratic presidential nomination in 1848, Buchanan retired to Wheatland, his Pennsylvania estate.

Buchanan tried twice more for the Democratic nomination. He failed in 1852, but President Pierce appointed him U.S. minister to Great Britain the following year. In 1856, Buchanan finally achieved his long-sought goal. His experience as a senator, cabinet member, and diplomat helped him win the nomination, but there were other factors. Although he was a Northerner, Buchanan was popular with Southern Democrats for his proslavery views.

In the election, Buchanan faced a new challenge: the Republican Party. Founded in 1854 by antislavery politicians from several parties, the Republicans nominated army officer and explorer John C. Frémont. Buchanan defeated Frémont and Know-Nothing candidate Millard Fillmore, but the election results showed that the nation was splitting apart over slavery. Buchanan won every slave state except Maryland. Frémont, however, won eleven of the sixteen free states, while Buchanan won only five.

James Buchanan is the only president who was a bachelor all his life. During his administration, Harriet Lane (1830–1903; above), the orphaned daughter of Buchanan's sister Jane, acted as White House hostess. She continued in this role after her marriage to Henry Elliot Johnson. Harriet Lane Johnson had a taste for art, and her collection of paintings found its way into the Smithsonian Institution's National Collection of Fine Arts. She also urged her uncle to adopt a fair policy toward the Native Americans.

In the 1856 campaign, Buchanan was known as a conservative and a compromiser. "I am not friendly to slavery in the abstract," he said, "[but] the rights of the South . . . are as much entitled to protection as those of any other position of the Union." This pro-Fillmore cartoon (opposite, top) shows Buchanan in second place, riding on the shoulders of incumbent Franklin Pierce. Frémont, stuck in the "Abolition Cesspool," brings up the rear.

The artist of this campaign poster from the election of 1856 made Buchanan look younger by giving the sixty-five-year-old candidate wavy hair and more youthful features. Buchanan enjoyed socializing and held lively parties as president, but some people were put off by his serious, dignified manner.

CRISIS AND SECESSION

When Buchanan took office in March 1857, the era of compromises was over. During his single term, the nation moved ever closer to civil war. Despite his wealth of experience in all aspects of politics, Buchanan was unable to hold the nation together.

In 1857, the controversy over slavery in the West reached the Supreme Court. In the *Dred Scott* decision, the court ruled that slavery was protected everywhere in the country, even in the new Western territories. That decision, combined with the continuing violence between pro- and antislavery settlers in Kansas, destroyed any support Buchanan had in the free states. The elections of 1858 brought many Republicans into Congress, further weakening the Democratic president's influence.

Buchanan didn't seek reelection in 1860. When Republican Abraham Lincoln won the election, Southern states began to secede from the Union, starting with South Carolina in December 1860. Although Buchanan believed secession was unconstitutional, he refused to use force against the seceding states. A gloomy Buchanan left office in March 1861, believing he was the last president of the United States. He lived to see the nation reunited, however, before his death on June 1, 1868, at the age of seventy-seven.

John Cabell Breckinridge (1821–75; above) was only thirty-six years old when he took the oath of office as vice president. Breckinridge, a Mexican War veteran and a former representative from Kentucky, ran for president in 1860 as the candidate of the Southern Democrats. Defeated in his bid for the White House, Breckinridge entered the Senate (he had been elected while still vice president). He was expelled for his pro-Southern sympathies after the Civil War broke out. He later served as a general in the Confederate Army.

The nation took a step closer to disunion in October 1859, when radical abolitionist John Brown launched a bloody raid on the federal arsenal at Harpers Ferry, Virginia, in hopes of sparking a slave uprising in the South. Brown and his handful of followers (opposite, top) were quickly defeated and captured, and he was hanged for treason in December. Brown's execution made him a martyr in the eyes of many antislavery Northerners.

One of the few bright spots of Buchanan's term was the arrival of the first Japanese diplomats in the United States. On May 17, 1860, President Buchanan received the diplomats in the White House, a scene depicted in this engraving (right) from Harper's Weekly. Among the gifts they brought was the world's largest porcelain bowl.

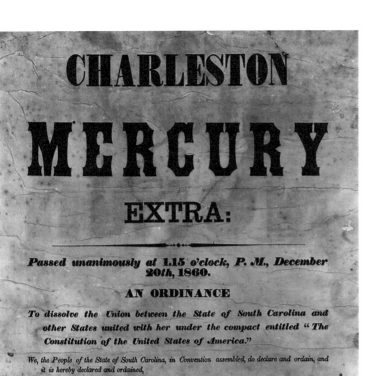

Buchanan was at a party when word of South Carolina's secession on December 20, 1860, reached him. The news stunned the president like a physical blow. "Please, won't someone call a carriage . . . I must go," he said before returning to the White House. The Charleston Mercury reprinted the state's ordinance of secession—which passed unanimously—in the special edition shown here (left).

"If you are as happy in entering the White House as I shall feel on returning to Wheatland, you are a happy man indeed," remarked Buchanan to Lincoln as the outgoing president left office. Wheatland, shown in this wood engraving (right), was the name of Buchanan's home near Lancaster, Pennsylvania.

Buchanan was a supporter of Abraham Lincoln during the Civil War, but many people despised the former president for his actions—or lack of them—in the years leading up to the conflict. His portrait in the Capitol was vandalized so many times that it was finally removed. Buchanan died in June 1868 and was buried in this tomb (right) in Woodward Hill Cemetery in Lancaster.

Resource Guide

Key to picture positions: (T) top, (C) center, (B) bottom; and in combinations: (TL) top left, (TR) top right, (BL) bottom left, (BR) bottom right, (RC) right center, (LC) left center.

Key to picture locations within the Library of Congress collections (and where available, photo negative numbers): P - Prints and Photographs Division; R - Rare Book Division; G - General Collections; MSS - Manuscript Division; G&M - Geography Division

PICTURES IN THIS VOLUME

2–3 view of Washington, P **4–5** half pound note, P **6–7** presidents, P **8–9** Map, G

Timeline: **10–11** Grand Canyon, G; cartoon, P, USZ62-809 **12–13** Van Buren, P; Oregon Trail, P, USZ62-8189 **14–15** TL, Taylor, USZ62-89292; BL, map, G&M, US 652; TR, Senate, P **16–17** raid, P, USZ62-33382; TR, Davis, G; RC, Harpers Ferry, P, USZ62-2893

Part I: **18–19** anecdotes, P **20–21** birthplace, P USZ62-39758; John Adams, P, USZ62-13002; Abigail Adams, P, USZ62-25768; **22–23** Louisa, P USZ62-25772; letter, MSS; ball, P, USZ62-10571 **24–25** Adams, P; Clay, P; cartoon, P, USZ62-9916 **26–27** debate, P, USZ62-32498; Adams, P, **28–29** TL, Rachel Robards, P, USZ62-25773; TR, cabins, P; BR, Jackson, P **30–31** BL, music, P; Jackson on horse, P; BR, meeting, P, USZ62-7811 **32–33** BL, White House, P, USZ62-1805; cartoon, P, USZ62-5745; BR, Jackson, P, USZ62-206 **34–35** TR, bug, P; bank cartoon, P, USZ62-809 **36–37** TL, boxing cartoon, P, USZ62-9650; TR, map, G&M; BR, assassination attempt, P, USZ62-2342 **38–39** TR, death of Jackson, P; Hermitage, P, USZ62-3550; **40–41** Hannah, P, USZ62-25776; cabinet meeting, P, USZ62-1580 **42–43** Johnson, P, USZ62-1887; TR, Van Buren, P; BR, inauguration, P, USZ62-7569 **44–45** TL, poster, P; TR, "Modern Colossus" cartoon, P; BR, cartoon, P, USZ62-00192; **46–47** TR, Anna, P, USZ62-25820; cabin, P, USZ62-25820 **48–49** Harrison, P; Fort, P **50–51** cartoon, P, USZ62-9592; Tecumseh, P; poster, P, USZ62-5550; kerchief, P, USZ62-32836 **52–53** portrait, P; tomb, P **54–55** TL, Letitia, P, USZ62-25779; Tyler, P, USZ62-276; BR, college, P, USZ62-57622 **56–57** TL, Julia, P, USZ62-25781; Princeton, P; house, P, USZ62-26726 *Part II:* **58–59** battle, P **60–61** Sarah, P; letter, MSS; young Polly, P, USZ62-9425; map, G&M **62–63** TL, Dallas, P, USZ62-10549; TR, poster, P; BR, cartoon, P, USZ62-1276 **64–65** C, Oregon City, P, USZ62-18184; TR, Slidell, P, LCB8184-10310 **66–67** TL, flag, P, LC-261-580; attack, P; tomb, P, USZ62-36921 **68–69** C, Seminoles, P; army, P **70–71** cartoon, P; Taylor on horse, P **72–73** Taylor, P; BR, deathbed, P, USZ62-25781 **74–75** TL, Abigail, P, USZ62-25784; C, Judge, P, USZ62-7550 **76–77** portrait, P, USZ62-13013; TR, procession, P, USZ62-763; ship, P **78–79** grave, P, USZ62-7348; house, P, USZ62-1828 **80–81** Hawthorne, P, LCBH824-4141; birthplace, P, USZ62-24830; June Pierce, P, USZ62-2586; Bowdoin, P, USZ62-2342 **82–83** Pierce, P; cartoon, USZ62-7184; banner, P **84–85** King, P, USZ62-50034; fight, P, USZ62-38851; poster, MSS **86–87** Johnston, P, USZ62-25788; sweepstakes, P, USZ62-7594; portrait, P **90–91** Breckinridge, P, USZ62-3975; raid, P, USZ62-38900; reception, P, USZ62-32022 **92–93** TL, broadside, MSS; TR, Wheatland, P, USZ62-1825; BR, Buchanan's tomb, P

SUGGESTED READING

BLASSINGAME, WYATT. *The Look-It-Up Book of Presidents.* New York: Random House, 1984.

CSINSKI, ALICE. *Andrew Jackson.* Chicago: Childrens Press, 1987.

DeGREGORIO, W. A. *The Complete Book of U.S. Presidents.* New York: Dembner Books, 1991.

MORSE, J. T. *John Quincy Adams.* New York: Chelsea House, 1981

OCHOA, GEORGE. *The Fall of Mexico City.* Englewood Cliffs: Silver Burdett Press, 1989.

WHITNEY, D. C. *The American Presidents,* 6th ed. New York: Doubleday, 1986.

Index

Page numbers in *italics* indicate illustrations